OPPOSING
VIEWPOINTS®
SERIES

Teens at Risk

Other Books of Related Interest:

"Congress shall make no law. . .abridging the freedom of speech, or of the press."

First Amendment to the U.S. Constitution

The basic foundation of our democracy is the First Amendment guarantee of freedom of expression. The Opposing Viewpoints Series is dedicated to the concept of this basic freedom and the idea that it is more important to practice it than to enshrine it.

OPPOSING
VIEWPOINTS®
SERIES

Teens at Risk

Christine Watkins, Book Editor

GREENHAVEN PRESS
A part of Gale, Cengage Learning

GALE
CENGAGE Learning™

Detroit • New York • San Francisco • New Haven, Conn • Waterville, Maine • London

GALE
CENGAGE Learning

Christine Nasso, *Publisher*
Elizabeth Des Chenes, *Managing Editor*

© 2009 Greenhaven Press, a part of Gale, Cengage Learning.

Gale and Greenhaven Press are registered trademarks used herein under license.

For more information, contact:
Greenhaven Press
27500 Drake Rd.
Farmington Hills, MI 48331-3535
Or you can visit our Internet site at gale.cengage.com

For product information and technology assistance, contact us at

Gale Customer Support, 1-800-877-4253
For permission to use material from this text or product, submit all requests online at www.cengage.com/permissions

Further permissions questions can be emailed to permissionrequest@cengage.com

Articles in Greenhaven Press anthologies are often edited for length to meet page requirements. In addition, original titles of these works are changed to clearly present the main thesis and to explicitly indicate the author's opinion. Every effort is made to ensure that Greenhaven Press accurately reflects the original intent of the authors. Every effort has been made to trace the owners of copyrighted material.

Cover photograph reproduced by permission of © Wizzard/Dreamstime.com

LIBRARY OF CONGRESS CATALOGING-IN-PUBLICATION DATA

Teens at risk / Christine Watkins, book editor.
   p. cm. -- (Opposing viewpoints)
   Includes bibliographical references and index.
   ISBN-13: 978-0-7377-4232-9 (hardcover)
   ISBN-13: 978-0-7377-4233-6 (pbk.)
   1. Teenagers with social disabilities--United States. 2. Problem youth--United States. 3. Juvenile delinquency--United States. 4. Teenage pregnancy--United States. 5. Teenagers--Substance use--United States. I. Watkins, Christine, 1951-
   HV1431.T437 2008
   362.7083--dc22
                                                            2008027870

Printed in the United States of America
1 2 3 4 5 6 7 12 11 10 09 08

Contents

Chapter 3: How Can Society Deal with Teenage Crime and Violence?

Chapter 4: How Can Teen Substance Abuse Be Reduced?

Why Consider Opposing Viewpoints?

> *"The only way in which a human being can make some approach to knowing the whole of a subject is by hearing what can be said about it by persons of every variety of opinion and studying all modes in which it can be looked at by every character of mind. No wise man ever acquired his wisdom in any mode but this."*
>
> John Stuart Mill

In our media-intensive culture it is not difficult to find differing opinions. Thousands of newspapers and magazines and dozens of radio and television talk shows resound with differing points of view. The difficulty lies in deciding which opinion to agree with and which "experts" seem the most credible. The more inundated we become with differing opinions and claims, the more essential it is to hone critical reading and thinking skills to evaluate these ideas. *Opposing Viewpoints* books address this problem directly by presenting stimulating debates that can be used to enhance and teach these skills. The varied opinions contained in each book examine many different aspects of a single issue. While examining these conveniently edited opposing views, readers can develop critical thinking skills such as the ability to compare and contrast authors' credibility, facts, argumentation styles, use of persuasive techniques, and other stylistic tools. In short, the *Opposing Viewpoints* series is an ideal way to attain the higher-level thinking and reading skills so essential in a culture of diverse and contradictory opinions.

In addition to providing a tool for critical thinking, *Opposing Viewpoints* books challenge readers to question their own strongly held opinions and assumptions. Most people form their opinions on the basis of upbringing, peer pressure, and personal, cultural, or professional bias. By reading carefully balanced opposing views, readers must directly confront new ideas as well as the opinions of those with whom they disagree. This is not to simplistically argue that everyone who reads opposing views will—or should—change his or her opinion. Instead, the series enhances readers' understanding of their own views by encouraging confrontation with opposing ideas. Careful examination of others' views can lead to the readers' understanding of the logical inconsistencies in their own opinions, perspective on why they hold an opinion, and the consideration of the possibility that their opinion requires further evaluation.

Evaluating Other Opinions

To ensure that this type of examination occurs, *Opposing Viewpoints* books present all types of opinions. Prominent spokespeople on different sides of each issue as well as well-known professionals from many disciplines challenge the reader. An additional goal of the series is to provide a forum for other, less known, or even unpopular viewpoints. The opinion of an ordinary person who has had to make the decision to cut off life support from a terminally ill relative, for example, may be just as valuable and provide just as much insight as a medical ethicist's professional opinion. The editors have two additional purposes in including these less known views. One, the editors encourage readers to respect others' opinions—even when not enhanced by professional credibility. It is only by reading or listening to and objectively evaluating others' ideas that one can determine whether they are worthy of consideration. Two, the inclusion of such viewpoints encourages the important critical thinking skill of objectively evaluating an author's credentials and bias. This evaluation will illuminate an author's reasons for taking a particular stance on an issue and will aid in readers' evaluation of the author's ideas.

It is our hope that these books will give readers a deeper understanding of the issues debated and an appreciation of the complexity of even seemingly simple issues when good and honest people disagree. This awareness is particularly important in a democratic society such as ours in which people enter into public debate to determine the common good. Those with whom one disagrees should not be regarded as enemies but rather as people whose views deserve careful examination and may shed light on one's own.

Thomas Jefferson once said that "difference of opinion leads to inquiry, and inquiry to truth." Jefferson, a broadly educated man, argued that "if a nation expects to be ignorant and free . . . it expects what never was and never will be." As individuals and as a nation, it is imperative that we consider the opinions of others and examine them with skill and discernment. The *Opposing Viewpoints* series is intended to help readers achieve this goal.

David L. Bender and Bruno Leone,
Founders

Introduction

"Poverty kills. It also maims and stunts the growth and eclipses the dreams of hundreds of millions of children around the world."

—*Children's Defense Fund*

Thirteen million children in the United States live in poverty. That means one out of every six children. Access to shelter, nutritious food, clean water, and health care are crucial to the well-being of children, yet millions of American families do not earn enough money to provide these basic necessities. Lack of resources can impair children's physical health and mental development, which in turn will handicap their ability to thrive in school, producing obstacle on top of obstacle into and throughout their adult lives. Children of poverty are more likely to become homeless, enter the foster care system, become victims of neglect or abuse, become teen parents, drop out of school, face unemployment, commit crimes, and continue the cycle by raising their own children in poverty. Poverty detrimentally impacts so many aspects of life that it is perhaps the most profound single factor that puts teens at risk.

The Children's Defense Fund reported in its *State of America's Children 2005* that "health is strongly correlated with income. Poor people are less healthy than those who are better off, whether the benchmark is mortality, the prevalence of acute or chronic diseases, or mental health." Beginning at birth—having received little, if any, prenatal care—many infants of disadvantaged parents are born with low birth weight. Physical disabilities, learning disabilities, and lower levels of intelligence are more prevalent among low-birth-weight children. Even if born at normal weight, disadvantaged children are still at risk for brain damage. Scientific research recently has shown that the high levels of stress hormones found in children under three years of age in families struggling to meet basic needs can actually hinder brain formation. "That is the age where all the connections are being made in the brain," said Lynda Gavioli, executive director of the Children's Coalition for Northeast Louisiana. "Later on in life, you can't go back and reconnect."

Environmental hazards associated with poverty also put teens at risk for poor health. Low-income youth have greater exposure to lead and are more than five times as likely to have elevated levels of lead in their blood than those from higher-income families. Lead poisoning can cause behavior problems, such as aggression and fighting, anxiety, social withdrawal and depression, stunted growth, hearing loss, impaired blood production, headaches, lower intelligence, and toxic effects on the kidneys. Teens in lower-income families often have a greater risk of exposure to allergens and mold, which increases the risk of asthma. They also generally experience a greater prevalence of obesity than those financially better off. This could be a result of living in dangerous neighborhoods where walking and playing outdoors can be life-threatening, and because foods high in calories, fats, and sugars tend to be more affordable and more easily obtained than foods of higher nutritional value. Obesity puts teens at risk for heart disease, high blood pressure, and stroke.

Poor health—whether it be mental, physical, or emotional—puts impoverished teens at an immediate disadvantage upon entering high school. To make matters worse, their moms or dads may be working multiple jobs just to meet basic needs, leaving these teens without the support and attention that learning demands. Struggling in school and left home alone after school, many underprivileged youth decide it is easier to simply give up and drop out. According to the

National Center for Education Statistics, low-income students are six times more likely to drop out of school than those from wealthy families. And the statistics regarding the future for high school dropouts are alarming: 72 percent are more likely to be unemployed than those who graduate; dropouts are three-and-a-half times more likely to be incarcerated; and of state prison inmates, 75 percent are dropouts. According to a study by a team of researchers from Northeastern University in Boston, over 5.5 million children nationwide are not in school and not working. "This army of uneducated, jobless young people, disconnected in most instances from society's mainstream, is restless and unhappy and poses a severe long-term threat to the nation's well-being on many fronts," wrote Bob Herbert in his 2003 *New York Times* article, "Young, Jobless, Hopeless."

It is difficult enough for children from stable families with adequate financial resources to cope with the pressures and risks in today's society, but for poor and underserved youth, the stress often proves debilitating. In their search for structure, protection, self-esteem, and a sense of belonging, underprivileged youth are susceptible to gangs and frequently get involved in a life of drug dealing, firearms trafficking, and violence. As a result, poor youth are at great risk of entering the juvenile justice system or, even worse, the adult criminal justice system, where they receive little sympathy or support from the American public. And once in the system, these juvenile offenders face almost insurmountable odds against returning to the community and becoming productive members. Will Okun, a Chicago school teacher with many students from low-income homes, wrote,

> It is easy to write off gang members. In my school, they are
> often hard, violent, disrespectful, indifferent, ignorant, hostile, agitated, boisterous, and confrontational. But sometimes
> you get a glimpse behind the steely façade and realize that

many of these gang members are just scared, angry teenagers who have raised themselves and are trying to navigate an adult world on their own.

The plight of impoverished teens grows worse every day because poverty continues to increase. Consider this: every thirty-five seconds a child is born into poverty. However, poverty is not the only factor that puts teens at risk; other factors include drug and alcohol abuse, sexual relationships, violent media images, and emotional stress. The authors in *Opposing Viewpoints: Teens at Risk* discuss how society can best deal with the many risks that teens face in today's world in such chapters as: What Factors Put Teens at Risk? How Can the Adverse Consequences of Teenage Sex and Pregnancy Be Reduced? How Can Society Deal with Teenage Crime and Violence? and How Can Teen Substance Abuse Be Reduced?

What Factors Put Teens at Risk?

Chapter Preface

It used to be that being a chubby kid meant enduring fat jokes and ridicule. But these days, experts recognize that the problems resulting from being overweight as a child are far more serious than hurt feelings. They can actually be life threatening. In fact, some of today's children may live two to five years less than their parents because of the consequences of obesity. According to the U.S. Surgeon General, overweight and obesity have reached epidemic proportions—more than 9 million children between the ages of six and nineteen are overweight. Obese children are at risk of developing such serious health disorders as insulin resistance and diabetes, high cholesterol, high blood pressure, heart disease, joint problems and osteoarthritis, sleep apnea, respiratory problems, and even cancer. As an example, in 2007 a seventeen-year-old girl who was five-feet one-inch tall, weighed 310 pounds, and had a fifty-inch waist died from type-2 diabetes. Taken together, overweight and obesity represent the second leading preventable cause of death in the United States.

Obesity is defined as an excessive accumulation and storage of fat, and can be determined by the ratio of weight to height, called the Body Mass Index (BMI). Heredity and lifestyle are major factors in a child's weight. A 2004 study reported that 48 percent of children with overweight parents became overweight themselves. Individual hormonal function also plays an important role in weight gain. However, adolescents generally gain weight because of poor eating habits and not enough physical activity. Public health officials believe that the environment surrounding kids today—with the emphasis on watching television, playing video games, socializing through the Internet, and eating high-fat fast foods—is a significant threat to health. As Dr. Sharon Alger, head of Albany

Medical Center's Northeast Center for Eating Disorders, said, "Genetics loads the gun. And the environment pulls the trigger."

In order to prevent young people from becoming overweight or obese, it is important to educate them about healthy exercise-oriented behaviors and effective weight-control strategies. Unhealthy weight-loss strategies—such as crash diets that severely restrict caloric intake and fad diets that allow only specific foods—have been proven to be ineffective and can actually lead to other physical and emotional complications. Simply put, teens should be encouraged to make lifestyle changes that focus on eating healthy foods in appropriate portions and exercising more to burn off the calories consumed. As an added incentive, a Harvard study found that when people lose weight through lifestyle changes, their weight loss can be contagious; chances are that their close friends and relatives will also lose weight.

Obesity is a serious, chronic disease that threatens teens' lives. The authors in the following chapter discuss other factors that put teens at risk.

"*There is now biological evidence that adolescents do not have the same ability as adults to make sound decisions and to prevent impulsive behavior.*"

The Adolescent Brain Puts Teens at Risk

Adam Ortiz

In the following viewpoint, Adam Ortiz explains that the brain of an adolescent is in a developing state and does not reach maturity until the approximate age of twenty-two. Specifically, the prefrontal cortex—the part of the brain that controls impulses and anticipates consequences—is underdeveloped in teenagers, which leads them to react to circumstances impulsively and aggressively instead of rationally. Thus, through no fault of their own, teenagers' brains put them at risk when making decisions. Adam Ortiz, a Soros Criminal Justice Fellow, wrote this article for the Juvenile Justice Center of the American Bar Association.

As you read, consider the following questions:

1. According to the viewpoint, what is the substance that the brain overproduces during adolescence that is detected through magnetic resonance imagining (MRI)?

2. According to the author, even the most sophisticated-appearing teenagers rely heavily on what part of the brain?

3. What does Ortiz claim is the hormone closely associated with aggression that has a dramatic effect on teenagers?

A long with everything else in the body, the brain changes significantly during adolescence. In the last five years [1998–2003], scientists have discovered that adolescent brains are far less developed than previously believed.

The human brain has been called the most complex three-pound mass in the known universe—and for good reason—it has literally billions of connections among its parts.

The largest part of the brain is called the frontal lobe. A small area of the frontal lobe called the prefrontal cortex, located behind the forehead, controls the most advanced functions. This part, often referred to as the "CEO" [chief executive officer] of the body, provides us with our advanced level of consciousness. It allows us to prioritize thoughts, imagine, think in the abstract, anticipate consequences, plan, and control impulses.

Brain Development

Researchers at UCLA [University of California, Los Angeles], Harvard Medical School and the National Institute of Mental Health have teamed up in a massive project to "map" the development of the brain from childhood to adulthood.

These scientists are utilizing advances in magnetic resonance imaging (MRI) which provides three-dimensional images of the body without the use of radiation (as in an x-ray). This breakthrough allows scientists to scan children safely numerous times over many years.

What came as a surprise to scientists was the discovery that the brain undergoes an intense overproduction of gray matter (the tissue that does the "thinking") during adolescence. Then, a period of "pruning" takes over, where gray matter is shed and discarded.

This process is similar to pruning the branches of a tree: cutting branches in some places stimulates growth overall.

The pruning process has been described as a "massive loss of brain tissue" by Paul Thompson, a member of the UCLA research team. Tissue is lost at a rate of 1 to 2% per year.

The pruning process is accompanied by myelination, a process in which the brain's white matter, or "insulation," focuses, refines and makes the brain's operation more efficient. The pace and severity of these changes, which continue until one's early 20s, have been carefully scrutinized by researchers. These changes mean that the brain is still developing.

Dr. Elizabeth Sowell, a member of the UCLA brain research team, has led studies of brain development from adolescence to adulthood (roughly ages 12 through 22). She writes that the frontal lobe undergoes the most change during adolescence—by far. It is also the last part of the brain to develop.

Both the pruning and the insulation process are critical to the brain's development. Insulation affects the speed and quality of brain activity while pruning and the development of gray matter contribute to overall cognitive functioning, including the ability to reason effectively.

Biology and Behavior

These correlations are providing new perspectives to the old question: "Why do teens behave the way they do?"

The answers to this question have widespread implications in the fields of education, mental illness, and juvenile justice, and were the centerpiece of a May 2000 White House Conference titled "Raising Responsible and Resourceful Youth."

Jay Giedd, the lead researcher on the subject at the National Institute of Mental Health, explained to PBS's *Frontline* that during adolescence the "part of the brain that is helping

Education and Intervention Programs Are Wasted on Teenagers

A new [2007] review of adolescent brain research suggests that society is wasting billions of dollars on education and intervention programs to dissuade teens from dangerous activities, because their immature brains are not yet capable of avoiding risky behaviors.

The analysis, by Temple University psychologist Laurence Steinberg, says stricter laws and policies limiting their behaviors would be more effective than education programs.

"We need to rethink our whole approach to preventing teen risk," says Steinberg. . . .

"Adolescents are at an age where they do not have full capacity to control themselves," he says. "As adults, we need to do some of the controlling."

Sharon Jayson,
"Expert: Risky Teen Behavior Is All in the Brain,"
USAToday.com, April 4, 2007.
www.usatoday.com/news/health/2007-04-04-teen-brain_IV.htm.

organization, planning and strategizing is not done being built yet. . . . It's sort of unfair to expect them to have adult levels of organizational skills or decision making before their brain is finished being built."

Connections to Disorders and Culpability

Dr. Deborah Yurgelun-Todd of Harvard Medical School is one of the chief researchers on the relation between brain development and cognitive deficiencies. She says that the underdevelopment of the frontal lobe makes adolescents "more prone to react with 'gut instinct.'" She says that the tendency to use the part of the brain called the amygdale (responsible for 'gut reactions') instead of the prefrontal cortex (responsible for reasoning) continues until adulthood, when individuals are able to respond more maturely.

MRI scans have shown that even the most sophisticated-appearing teenagers rely heavily on the amygdala, an instinctual part of the brain. Also, males use these 'instinctual' parts of the brain much more than females as the male frontal lobe develops more slowly than that of the female's.

Dr. Ruben C. Gur, neuropsychologist and Director of the Brain Behavior Laboratory at the University of Pennsylvania, explains that the frontal lobe is "involved in behavioral facets germane to many aspects of criminal culpability. Perhaps most relevant is the involvement of these brain regions in the control of aggression and other impulses. . . . If the neural substrates of these behaviors have not reached maturity before adulthood, it is unreasonable to expect the behaviors themselves to reflect mature thought processes."

Simply put, there is now biological evidence that adolescents do not have the same ability as adults to make sound decisions and to prevent impulsive behavior.

Dr. Gur writes: "The evidence now is strong that the brain does not cease to mature until the early 20s in those relevant parts that govern impulsivity, judgment, planning for the future, foresight of consequences, and other characteristics that make people morally culpable. . . . Indeed, age 21 or 22 would be closer to the 'biological' age of maturity."

Other Changes in the Body

In addition to the profound physical changes of the brain, adolescents also undergo dramatic hormonal and emotional changes.

One of the hormones having the most dramatic effect on the body is testosterone, closely associated with aggression, which increases its levels tenfold.

Emotionally, an adolescent "is really both part child and part adult," according to professor and author Melvin Lewis. Normal emotional development includes a period of self-searching, where the adolescent tries to grow out of the child. This involves a conflict between building identity and facing childlike insecurities. The well-known behaviors associated with this process include self-absorption, a powerful need for privacy, mood swings, dressing uniquely, and participating in forms of escapism such as video games, music, talking on the phone, and riskier behaviors such as using drugs or engaging in sexual activity.

Development and Delinquency

The turmoil often associated with these changes sometimes results in poor decisions and desperate behaviors.

Studies find that 20 to 30 percent of high school students consider suicide, and that suicide is the third-leading cause of death among teenagers, occurring once every two hours—well over 4,000 times a year, according to the US Surgeon General.

Running away from home is also common, as the General Accounting Office estimates 1.3 million kids are on the street each year.

The US Office of National Drug Control Policy estimates that 10.8 percent of persons between ages 12 and 18 used an illicit drug "in the past month" (well above the national average of 7.1 percent of the population at large) and nearly a third of adolescents used alcohol.

Also, illegal acts are more common during adolescence than during any other time of life. Estimates of the proportion of males who have been arrested before the age of 18 hover around 25%. This peak in criminal activity during adolescence is "quite stable across different social contexts" and "is present in all of the cultures studied to date."

Triggers to Violent Behavior

Research also shows that certain stressful experiences can trigger violent behavior, like a spark to flammable material. The American Academy of Pediatrics has identified several risk factors that can trigger violence in adolescents including being witness to domestic violence or substance abuse within the family, being poorly or inappropriately supervised, and being the victim of physical or sexual assault, among other things.

It should come as no surprise that juveniles who commit murder come from environments rife with these triggers. In 1987, Dr. Dorothy Otnow Lewis of New York University led comprehensive diagnostic evaluations of 14 juveniles on death row (at that time, 40 percent) in four states. She found that nine had major neuropsychological disorders and seven had psychotic disorders since early childhood. Twelve reported having been brutally abused physically or sexually, and five reported having been sodomized by relatives.

Other common characteristics included suffering trauma to the head and IQ scores under 90 (only two did better). Only three had average reading abilities, and another three had learned to read on death row. Lewis also found that many of these dysfunctions were not presented to juries due to poor representation or the juvenile withholding or downplaying these facts out of embarrassment or bad judgment.

Dr. Lewis' primary findings were later corroborated by [D.A.] Robinson and [O.H.] Stephens. They found that two thirds of all juveniles sentenced to death had backgrounds of abuse, profound psychological disturbances, low IQ, indigence, and/or intensive substance abuse.

"Less than Adult"

New scientific research confirms that adolescence is a time of transition. The adolescent is not an adult, and is subject to great limitations in judgment and maturity.

For social and biological reasons, teens have increased difficulty making mature decisions and understanding the consequences of their actions. Research suggests that these limitations persist until the early 20s.

Often, adolescents *grow out of* these less mature ways of dealing with problems, including destructive behavior. Studies show that more than half of all youths that pass through the juvenile justice system do not return.

This understanding does not excuse adolescents from punishments for violent crime, but it clearly lessens their culpability. This is the premise beneath society's across-the-board restrictions on voting rights, alcohol and tobacco consumption and serving in the armed forces. Indeed, this is why we refer to those under 18 as "minors" and "juveniles"—because, in so many respects, they are *less than adult.*

"There's enough data that clearly indicates that [game violence] is a problem. And it's not just a problem for kids with behavior disorders."

Violent Video Games Put Teens at Risk

Kristin Kalning

In the following viewpoint, Kristin Kalning discusses a study that was performed to determine how the brains of adolescents react after playing violent video games. Immediately following play sessions, children were given brain scans, which revealed a negative effect on the brains of those teens that played games with violent content. Although some members of the game development community disparage the importance of the results, Vince Mathews, the principle investigator on the study, believes that parents need to be aware of the relationship between violent video gaming and brain function. Kristin Kalning is the games editor at MSNBC.

As you read, consider the following questions:

1. Brain scans that were performed on kids immediately after they played a violent video game revealed an increase in what type of brain activity, according to the author?

2. What does Kalning claim are the areas of the brain that show a decrease in brain activity in children following video game activity?

3. According to research director Larry Ley as stated in the viewpoint, what was the purpose of the study?

Can video games make kids more violent? A new study employing state-of-the-art brain-scanning technology says that the answer may be yes.

Researchers at the Indiana University School of Medicine say that brain scans of kids who played a violent video game showed an increase in emotional arousal—and a corresponding decrease of activity in brain areas involved in self-control, inhibition and attention.

Does this mean that your teenager will feel an uncontrollable urge to go on a shooting rampage after playing "Call of Duty"?

Brains Are Scanned

Vince Mathews, the principal investigator on the study, hesitates to make that leap. But he says he does think that the study should encourage parents to look more closely at the types of games their kids are playing.

"Based on our results, I think parents should be aware of the relationship between violent video-game playing and brain function."

Mathews and his colleagues chose two action games to include in their research—one violent the other not.

The first game was the high-octane but non-violent racing game "Need for Speed: Underground." The other was the ultra-violent first-person shooter "Medal of Honor: Frontline."

The team divided a group of 44 adolescents into two groups, and randomly assigned the kids to play one of the two games. Immediately after the play sessions, the children were given MRIs [magnetic resonance imaging scans] of their brains.

The scans showed a negative effect on the brains of the teens who played "Medal of Honor" for 30 minutes. That same effect was not present in the kids who played "Need for Speed."

The only difference? Violent content.

What's not clear is whether the activity picked up by the MRIs indicates a lingering—or worse, permanent—effect on the kids' brains.

And it's also not known what effect longer play times might have. The scope of this study was 30 minutes of play, and one brain scan per kid, although further research is in the works.

OK. But what about violent TV shows? Or violent films? Has anyone ever done a brain scan of kids that have just watched a violent movie?

Someone has, John P. Murray, a psychology professor at Kansas State University, conducted a very similar experiment, employing the same technology used in Mathews' study. His findings are similar.

Kids in his study experienced increased emotional arousal when watching short clips from the boxing movie "Rocky IV."

Parents Should Be Aware of the Study Results

So, why is everyone picking on video games? Probably because there's a much smaller body of research on video games. They

Brain Scan Results

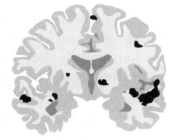
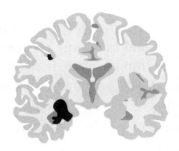

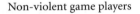

Non-violent game players   Violent game players

In a recent research study, adolescents played two different types of video games for 30 minutes. Teens that played the violent game (right) showed increased activity in the amygdala, which is involved in emotional arousal.

TAKEN FROM: Radiological Society of North America.

just haven't been around as long as TV and movies, so the potential effects on children are a bigger unknown. That's a scary thing for a parent.

Larry Ley, the director and coordinator of research for the Center for Successful Parenting, which funded Mathews' study, says the purpose of the research was to help parents make informed decisions.

"There's enough data that clearly indicates that [game violence] is a problem," he says. "And it's not just a problem for kids with behavior disorders."

But not everyone is convinced that this latest research adds much to the debate—particularly the game development community. One such naysayer is Doug Lowenstein, president of the Entertainment Software Association [ESA].

"We've seen other studies in this field that have made dramatic claims but turn out to be less persuasive when objectively analyzed."

The ESA has a whole section of its Web site dedicated to the topic of video game violence, which would suggest that they get asked about it—a lot.

And they've got plenty of answers at the ready for the critics who want to lay school shootings or teen aggression at the feet of the game industry. Several studies cited by the ESA point to games' potential benefits for developing decision-making skills or bettering reaction times.

Ley, however, argues such studies aren't credible because they were produced by "hired guns" funded by the multi-billion-dollar game industry.

"We're not trying to sell [parents] anything," he says. "We don't have a product. The video game industry does."

Increasingly parents are more accepting of video game violence, chalking it up to being a part of growing up.

"I was dead-set against violent video games," says Kelley Windfield, a Sammamish, Wa.–based mother of two. "But my husband told me I had to start loosening up."

Laura Best, a mother of three from Clovis, Calif., says she looks for age-appropriate games for her 14-year-old son, Kyle. And although he doesn't play a lot of games, he does tend to gravitate towards shooters like "Medal of Honor." But she isn't concerned that Kyle will become aggressive as a result.

"That's like saying a soccer game or a football game will make a kid more aggressive," she says. "It's about self-control, and you've got to learn it."

Ley says he believes further research, for which the Center for Successful Parenting is trying to arrange, will prove a cause-and-effect relationship between game violence and off-screen aggression.

But for now, he says, the study released last week [on November 29, 2006] gives his organization the ammunition it needs to prove that parents need to be more aware of how kids are using their free time.

"Let's quit using various Xboxes as babysitters instead of doing healthful activities," says Ley, citing the growing epidemic of childhood obesity in the United States.

And who, really, can argue with that?

| *"Violent video games have been around since 1991, yet clear evidence of any harm has yet to emerge."*

Violent Video Games Have Not Been Proven to Harm Teens

Benjamin Radford

The author of the following viewpoint contends that the stigma attached to video games—that gaming is unhealthy and can even lead to violence—is unproven and unwarranted. Gaming is a cultural phenomenon that has captured the interest of teens as well as adults: the average video gamer is thirty years old. The author examines the lack of scientific validity of the studies that insist upon a correlation between violence and videogames. Benjamin Radford is managing editor of Skeptical Inquirer *science magazine; he previously wrote about the video game violence debate in his book, "Media Makers: How Journalists, Activists, and Advertisers Mislead Us."*

As you read, consider the following questions:

1. Has video game violence resulted in an increase in violent crime?

Radford, Benjamin, "Reality Check on Video Game Violence," livescience.com, December 4, 2005. Reproduced by permission.

2. What does the study by Craig Anderson and Karen Dill, which examines the link between aggression and violent video games, prove?

3. The author lists two other forms of entertainment that were accused of corrupting youth. What were they?

The debate about violence in entertainment has surfaced once again.

In late November, a media watchdog group, the National Institute on Media and the Family (NIMF), issued its annual report on video games. Not surprisingly, the institute was not happy with what it found: animated violence, profanity, and some sexual content. (Its latest report even includes a made-up word to describe the video violence, claming that "killographic and sexually explicit games are still making their way into the hands . . . of underage players.")

The findings caught the attention and support of several politicians, including Senators Joe Lieberman and Hillary Rodham Clinton, both of whom promised to enact legislation to stem the threat posed by video games.

Yet before rushing to craft new laws, we should make sure there is a problem to fix. Moving from the realm of advocacy and politics into science and evidence, several issues should be considered.

While many teens do play video games, including some violent ones, the games are hardly kids' stuff: the average video gamer is 30 years old. Most "Mature" or "Adult" rated video games are purchased—and played—by adults.

Relationship to Violence

While some studies claim that violent entertainment may be linked in some way to violent behavior, many other studies contradict that assertion. Where are the mountains of evidence demonstrating the harmful effects of fake violence? Richard Rhodes, a writer for *Rolling Stone*, tackled that question and found that the alleged mountains of evidence are really molehills—and shaky ones at that.

The approximately 200 studies on media violence are remarkable primarily for their inconsistency and weak conclusions. Some studies show a correlation between television and violence; others don't. Some find that violent programming can increase aggressiveness; another finds that "Mr. Rogers' Neighborhood" does. Several studies, including the most-cited ones, are deeply flawed methodologically. Still, those fighting media depictions of violence cite the studies and ignore their lack of scientific validity. Rhodes notes that "The research no more supports the consensus on media violence than it supported the conclusions of the eugenics consensus eighty years ago that there are superior and inferior 'races,' with White Northern Europeans at the top."

The assertion that video games make people violent got a boost in May of 2000, when the American Psychological Association issued a press release saying that violent video games can increase aggression. That conclusion was taken from a study by two researchers, Craig Anderson of Iowa State University and Karen Dill of Lenoir-Rhyne College in North Carolina. The pair claimed that they had found a link between violent video games and aggression.

Accuracy of Studies Linking Videogames and Violence

Yet an examination of what the researchers actually found shows how tentative their conclusions are. The study seems to show some association between the playing of violent video games and concurrent aggressive behavior and delinquency. Yet, as any social sciences or psychology student knows, correlation does not imply causation.

One critic of the study, British psychologist Guy Cumberbatch, noted, "[F]inding that people who enjoy violent media

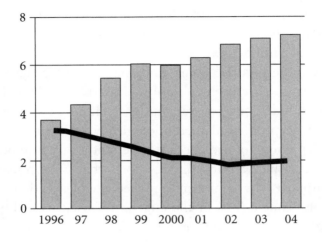

Violent Crime, Decreased as Computer and Video Game Sales Soared, 1996–2004

■ Total violent crime offences (in millions)

▨ Computer and video-game sales ($ in billions)

TAKEN FROM: U.S. Dept. of Justice: Office of Juvenile Justice and Delinquency Prevention / The Entertainment Software Association.

may also be aggressive is tantamount to observing that those who play football also enjoy watching it on television. 'The correlational nature of [this] study means that causal statements are risky at best,' the authors admit. . . . All in all, Anderson and Dill's new evidence is exceptionally weak, and in its one-sided approach it has a depressingly familiar ring to it. . . . [S]tudies to date have been notably biased towards seeking evidence of harm. This 'blame game' may be fun for some researchers to play, and knee-jerk reactions such as the APA's press release may be media-friendly. But we deserve better."

Effects of Videogame Violence

Perhaps most tellingly, video game critics fail to show where, exactly, the real-world evidence of harm lies. Assuming that teens are being exposed to bad language and animated violence, so what? Daily teen life involves some profanity, adult themes, and violent entertainment. Has the sexual material resulted in an increase in teen sex? No; the National Center for Health Statistics reported last year that fewer teens are engaging in sexual activity than in the past, and the rate dropped significantly between 1995 and 2002.

Has the video violence resulted in an increase in violent crime? No; on Oct. 17, 2005, the FBI released figures showing that the U.S. violent crime rate declined again last year. In fact, violent crime has dropped significantly over the past twenty years—just as video games have become more violent. The NIMF and Senator Lieberman even decried "graphic scenes of cannibalism" in video games.

Should America brace itself for a rise in teen cannibalism? *Violent video games have been around since 1991, yet clear evidence of any harm has yet to emerge.*

Violence in the Media

Amid all the concern over the violence that teens and kids see in their video games, television shows, and films, one simple fact is often overlooked: Violence and killing is considered mainstream entertainment by most Americans.

Multiple murders are entertainment every single night. Top-rated television drama shows routinely involve killings and death, from "Law & Order" to "CSI" to "The Sopranos" to "ER." While many of the murders that entertain us are fictional, others aren't. Newsmagazine shows such as "Dateline NBC" and "48 Hours" regularly feature real-life murders packaged as entertainment mysteries.

Blaming entertainment for social ills is nothing new, of course; Elvis Presley was accused of corrupting America's youth with lewd hip gyrations in the 1950s, for example, and in 1880s London the play "Dr. Jekyll and Mr. Hyde" was blamed for encouraging Jack the Ripper in his crimes. In sci-

ence, outside the agenda enclaves, the effects of violent entertainment and video games on behavior is very much an open
question.

> "Whether the incidence of teen depression is actually increasing, or we're just becoming more aware of it, the fact is that depression strikes teenagers far more often than most people think."

Depression Puts Teens at Risk

Helpguide.org

As the Helpguide organization mentions in the following viewpoint, depression among teenagers is more widespread than many people realize. The organization describes the signs and symptoms of adolescent depression and offers advice on how best to help and support the depressed teen. The benefits and risks involving the use of antidepressants are also discussed. Helpguide is an organization that provides information to understand, prevent, and resolve health challenges.

As you read, consider the following questions:

1. According to the Helpguide organization, how do most teenagers suffering from depression get the treatment they need?

Melinda Smith, Suzanne Barston, Jaelline Jaffe, Lisa Flores Dumke and Jeanne Segal, "Teen Depression: A Guide for Parents and Teachers," Helpguide.org, November 15, 2007. Copyright © 2008 All rights reserved. Reprinted with permission from http://www.helpguide.org.

2. What is the third leading cause of death for fifteen- to twenty-four-year-olds, according to the Centers for Disease Control and Prevention?

3. According to the authors, what depression medication do researchers believe might interfere with the development of an adolescent's brain?

Teenage depression isn't just bad moods and occasional melancholy. Depression is a serious problem that impacts every aspect of a teen's life. Left untreated, teen depression can lead to problems at home and school, drug abuse, self-loathing—even irreversible tragedy such as homicidal violence or suicide. Fortunately, teenage depression can be treated. . . .

There are as many misconceptions about teen depression as there are about teenagers in general. Yes, the teen years are tough, but most teens balance the requisite angst with good friendships, success in school or outside activities, and the development of a strong sense of self. Occasional bad moods or acting out is to be expected, but depression is something different. Depression can destroy the very essence of a teenager's personality, causing an overwhelming sense of sadness, despair, or anger.

Whether the incidence of teen depression is actually increasing, or we're just becoming more aware of it, the fact is that depression strikes teenagers far more often than most people think. And although depression is highly treatable, experts say only 20% of depressed teens ever receive help.

Unlike adults, who have the ability to seek assistance on their own, teenagers usually must rely on parents, teachers, or other caregivers to recognize their suffering and get them the treatment they need. So if you have an adolescent in your life, it's important to learn what teen depression looks like and what to do if you spot the warning signs.

Signs and Symptoms of Teen Depression

Teenagers face a host of pressures, from the changes of puberty to questions about who they are and where they fit in. The natural transition from child to adult can also bring parental conflict as teens start to assert their independence. With all this drama, it isn't always easy to differentiate between depression and normal teenage moodiness. Making things even more complicated, teens with depression do not necessarily appear sad, nor do they always withdraw from others. For some depressed teens, symptoms of irritability, aggression, and rage are more prominent.

If you're unsure if an adolescent in your life is depressed or just "being a teenager," consider how long the symptoms have been present, how severe they are, and how different the teen is acting from his or her usual self. While some "growing pains" are to be expected as teenagers grapple with the challenges of growing up, dramatic, long-lasting changes in personality, mood, or behavior are red flags of a deeper problem.

Depression in teens can look very different from depression in adults. The following symptoms of depression are more common in teenagers than in their adult counterparts:

1. *Irritable or angry mood*—As noted above, irritability, rather than sadness, is often the predominant mood in depressed teens. A depressed teenager may be grumpy, hostile, easily frustrated, or prone to angry outbursts.

2. *Unexplained aches and pains*—Depressed teens frequently complain about physical ailments such as headaches or stomachaches. If a thorough physical exam does not reveal a medical cause, these aches and pains may indicate depression.

3. *Extreme sensitivity to criticism*—Depressed teens are plagued by feelings of worthlessness, making them extremely vulnerable to criticism, rejection, and failure. This is a particular problem for "over-achievers."

4. *Withdrawing from some, but not all people*—While adults tend to isolate themselves when depressed, teenagers usually keep up at least some friendships. However, teens with depression may socialize less than before, pull away from their parents, or start hanging out with a different crowd. . . .

Suicide Warning Signs in Teenagers

An alarming and increasing number of teenagers attempt and succeed at suicide. According to the Centers for Disease Control and Prevention (CDC), suicide is the third leading cause of death for 15- to 24-year-olds. For the overwhelming majority of suicidal teens, depression or another psychological disorder plays a primary role. In depressed teens who also abuse alcohol or drugs, the risk of suicide is even greater.

Because of the very real danger of suicide, teenagers who are depressed should be watched closely for any signs of suicidal thoughts or behavior. The warning signs include:

1. Talking or joking about committing suicide.

2. Saying things like, "I'd be better off dead," "I wish I could disappear forever," or "There's no way out."

3. Speaking positively about death or romanticizing dying ("If I died, people might love me more").

4. Writing stories and poems about death, dying, or suicide.

5. Engaging in reckless behavior or having a lot of accidents resulting in injury.

6. Giving away prized possessions.

7. Saying goodbye to friends and family as if for good.

8. Seeking out weapons, pills, or other ways to kill themselves.

Helping a Depressed Teenager

If you suspect that a teenager in your life is suffering from depression, take action right away. Depression is very damaging when left untreated, so don't wait and hope that the symptoms will go away. Even if you're unsure that depression is the issue, the troublesome behaviors and emotions you're seeing in your teenager are signs of a problem. Whether or not that problem turns out to be depression, it still needs to be addressed—the sooner the better.

The first thing you should do if you suspect depression is to talk to your teen about it. In a loving and non-judgmental way, share your concerns with your teenager. Let him or her know what specific signs of depression you've noticed and why they worry you. Then encourage your child to open up about what he or she is going through.

If your teen claims nothing is wrong, but has no explanation for what is causing the depressed behavior, you should trust your instincts. Remember that denial is a strong emotion. Furthermore, teenagers may not believe that what they're experiencing is the result of depression. If you see depression's warning signs, seek professional help. Neither you nor your teen is qualified to either diagnose depression or rule it out, so see a doctor or psychologist who can.

Visit the Family Doctor

Make an immediate appointment for your teen to see the family physician for a depression screening. Be prepared to give your doctor specific information about your teen's depression symptoms, including how long they've been present, how much they're affecting your child's daily life, and any patterns you've noticed. The doctor should also be told about any close relatives who have ever been diagnosed with depression or another mental health disorder.

As part of the depression screening, the doctor will give your teenager a complete physical exam and take blood

Effects of Teen Depression

The negative effects of teenage depression go far beyond a melancholy mood. Many rebellious and unhealthy behaviors or attitudes in teenagers are actually indications of depression. See the table below for some of the ways in which teens "act out" or "act in" in an attempt to cope with their emotional pain:

Untreated depression can lead to . . .

Eating disorders: Anorexia, bulimia, binge eating, and yo-yo dieting are often signs of unrecognized depression.

Internet addiction: Teens may go online to escape from their problems. But excessive computer use only increases their isolation and makes them more depressed.

Self-injury: Cutting, burning, and other kinds of self-mutilation are almost always associated with depression.

Reckless behavior: Depressed teens may engage in dangerous or high-risk behaviors, such as reckless driving, out-of-control drinking, and unsafe sex.

Violence: Some depressed teens (usually boys who are the victims of bullying) become violent. As in the case of the Columbine school massacre, self-hatred and a wish to die can erupt into violence and homicidal rage.

Suicide: Teens who are seriously depressed often think, speak of, make "attention-getting" attempts at suicide. Suicidal thoughts or behaviors should always be taken very seriously.

Helpguide.org,
"Teen Depression: A Guide for Parents and Teachers,"
November 15, 2007. www.helpguide.org/mental/depression_teen.htm.

samples to check for medical causes of your child's symptoms. In order to diagnose depression, other possible causes of your teen's symptoms must first be ruled out. The doctor will check for medical causes of the depression by giving your teenager a complete physical exam and running blood tests. The doctor may also ask your teen about other things that could be causing the symptoms, including heavy alcohol and drug use, a lack of sleep, a poor diet (especially one low in iron), and medications (including birth control pills and diet pills).

If there are no health problems that are causing your teenager's depression, ask your doctor to refer you to a psychologist or psychiatrist who specializes in children and adolescents. Depression in teens can be tricky, particularly when it comes to treatment options such as medication. A mental health professional with advanced training and a strong background treating adolescents is the best bet for your teenager's best care.

When choosing a specialist, always get your child's input. Teenagers are dependent on you for making many of their health decisions, so listen to what they're telling you. No one therapist is a miracle worker and no one treatment works for everyone. If your child feels uncomfortable or is just not 'connecting' with the psychologist or psychiatrist, ask for a referral to another provider that may be better suited to your teenager.

Expect a discussion with the specialist you've chosen about treatment possibilities for your son or daughter. There are a number of treatment options for depression in teenagers, including one-on-one talk therapy, group or family therapy, and medication.

Talk therapy is often a good initial treatment for mild to moderate cases of depression. Over the course of therapy, your teen's depression may resolve. If it doesn't, medication may be warranted. However, antidepressants should only be used as part of a broader treatment plan.

Use of Antidepressants

According to the National Institute of Mental Health:

> When medication is used, it should not be the only strategy. There are other services that you may want to investigate for your child. Family support services, educational classes, behavior management techniques, as well as family therapy and other approaches should be considered. If medication is prescribed, it should be monitored and evaluated regularly.

Unfortunately, some parents feel pushed into choosing antidepressant medication over other treatments that may be cost-prohibitive or time-intensive. However, unless your child is considered to be high risk for suicide (in which case medication and/or constant observation may be necessary), you have time to carefully weigh your options before committing to any one treatment.

Antidepressant medication can be helpful, particularly for severe cases of depression. However, medications always come with risks and side effects of their own. When it comes to antidepressant use in teenagers, there are a number of safety concerns that parents should be aware of. Before starting your child on medication, you should carefully weigh the potential benefits against the risks.

Antidepressants were designed and tested on adults, so their impact on the youthful, developing brain is not yet completely understood. Some researchers are concerned that the use of drugs such as Prozac in children and teens might interfere with normal brain development. Says neuroscientist Amir Raz, quoted in a June 2007 article in *Scientific American Mind*, "The human brain is developing exponentially when we are very young, and exposure to antidepressants may affect or influence the wiring of the brain, especially when it comes to certain elements that have to do with stress, emotion and the regulation of these."

Antidepressant medications may increase the risk of suicidal thinking and behavior in some teenagers. All antidepressants are required by the U.S. Food and Drug Administration (FDA) to carry a "black box" warning label about this risk in children and adolescents. In May 2007, the FDA recommended that the warning be expanded to include young adults from ages 18 to 24. The risk of suicide is particularly great during the first one to two months of antidepressant treatment.

Certain young adults are at an even greater risk for suicide when taking antidepressants, including teens with bipolar disorder, a family history of bipolar disorder, or a history of previous suicide attempts.

Teenagers on antidepressants should be closely monitored for any sign that the depression is getting worse. Warning signs include new or worsening symptoms of agitation, irritability, or anger. Unusual changes in behavior are also red flags.

According to FDA guidelines, after starting an antidepressant or changing the dose, your teenager should see their doctor:

1. Once a week for four weeks

2. Every 2 weeks for the next month

3. At the end of their 12th week taking the drug

4. More often if problems or questions arise

Supporting a Teen Through Treatment

As the depressed teenager in your life goes through treatment, the most important thing you can do is to let him or her know that you're there to listen and offer support. Now more than ever, your teenager needs to know that he or she is valued, accepted, and cared for.

1. *Be understanding.* Living with a depressed teenager can be difficult and draining. At times, you may experience exhaustion, rejection, despair, aggravation, or any other number of negative emotions. During this trying time, it's important to remember that your child is not being

difficult on purpose. Your teen is suffering, so do your best to be patient and understanding.

2. *Encourage physical activity.* Encourage your teenager to stay active. Exercise can go a long way toward relieving the symptoms of depression, so find ways to incorporate it into your teenager's day. Something as simple as walking the dog or going on a bike ride can be beneficial.

3. *Encourage social activity.* Isolation only makes depression worse, so encourage your teenager to see friends and praise efforts to socialize. Offer to take your teen out with friends or suggest social activities that might be of interest, such as sports, after-school clubs, or an art class.

4. *Stay involved in treatment.* Make sure your teenager is following all treatment instructions and going to therapy. It's especially important that your child takes any prescribed medication as instructed. Track changes in your teen's condition, and call the doctor if depression symptoms seem to be getting worse.

5. *Learn about depression.* Just like you would if your child had a disease you knew very little about, read up on depression so that you can be your own "expert." The more you know, the better equipped you'll be to help your depressed teen. Encourage your teenager to learn more about depression as well. Reading up on their condition can help depressed teens realize that they're not alone and give them a better understanding of what they're going through.

The road to your depressed teenager's recovery may be bumpy, so be patient. Rejoice in small victories and prepare for the occasional setback. Most importantly, don't judge yourself or compare your family to others. As long as you're doing your best to get your teen the necessary help, you're doing your job.

| "Children who are bullied often suffer from depression and low self-esteem well into adulthood." |

Bullying Puts Teens at Risk

Finessa Ferrell-Smith

In the following viewpoint, Finessa Ferrell-Smith discusses the problem of school bullying and the serious, sometimes lifelong consequences for both the bully and the victim. Research has shown that children who are bullied often experience low self-esteem, depression, feelings of loneliness, and difficulty making friends. And students who bully are likely to have poor grades, smoke cigarettes, drink alcohol, and commit crimes. Finessa Ferrell-Smith is a research analyst with the National Conference of State Legislatures' Children and Families Program.

As you read, consider the following questions:

1. According to the author, what is the universally understood definition of bullying?
2. As cited in the viewpoint, what are the three types of bullying among females?

3. According to research mentioned by the author, what effect does bullying have on academic achievement?

As the safety of U.S. schools has become an important public policy issue, interest in the problem of school bullying has intensified. New research indicates that this type of adolescent victimization occurs frequently, particularly in middle school grades, and can result in serious consequences for both bully and victim. In 2002, a report released by the U.S. Secret Service concluded that bullying played a significant role in many school shootings and that efforts should be made to eliminate bullying behavior.

Although the media often have focused on high-profile incidents of school violence, such as school shootings, it is also beginning to pay more attention to understanding why some kids bully others, what the consequences of this sort of victimization are and what can be done to stop it. John Stossel's [2002] ABC news special on bullying; Showtime's original movie, *Bang! Bang! You're Dead*; and the decision by Erika Harold, the [2003] reigning Miss America, to focus on bullying prevention have highlighted the role bullying plays in the broader picture of school violence and the growing importance of the issue.

As awareness of harassment, intimidation and hate in the school setting has grown, state legislatures have begun to address this problem as well. At least 16 states have passed anti-bullying laws, and similar measures were considered in 23 states in the 2001–2002 legislative sessions. Currently [2003], 14 legislatures are considering bills that address the issue of bullying.

Definitions of Bullying

Before legislatures were required to define bullying in more precise terms, characterizing "bullying" had largely been a question of individual judgment—"we know what it is when we see it." Bullying includes harassment, intimidation to varying degrees, taunting and ridicule. Sometimes, bullies are motivated by hate and bias, sometimes by cultural norms, peer pressure or the desire to retaliate. Bullying may occur within the context of initiation rituals and be labeled "hazing," or it can be overtly or implicitly about gender, constituting sexual harassment. Sometimes, there is no readily identifiable reason for bullying; when kids are asked who school bullies target, their answers can be disturbing precisely because they are not extraordinary: bullies pick on kids who are "weaker," "smaller," "funny looking," or "dumb."

Although no standard or universally understood definition of bullying exists, certain elements usually are present. The first element is a pattern of behavior over time—repeated exposure to intentional injury or discomfort inflicted by one or more students against another. This behavior may include physical contact, verbal assault, social ostracism, obscene gestures or other aggressive acts that cause the victim to feel fearful or distraught. More serious instances of bullying can result in physical injury or emotional trauma. A second common element is a perceived imbalance of power, which allows one student—or group of students—to victimize others.

Female Bullying

Although the traditional bullying model has been particularly male-centered and focused on physical aggression, more attention is being paid to bullying by girls. Boys generally bully in direct and physical ways; girls who bully often do so indirectly by teasing and spreading rumors.

Researchers in the area of female bullying suggest that there are three different types of adolescent female aggression: relational, indirect and social. Examples of relational aggression include damage or the threat of damage to a relationship, friendship or group inclusion; ignoring someone to punish or get one's way; and using negative body language or facial expressions. Indirect aggression allows the perpetrator to avoid confronting her target and makes it seem as though there has been no intent to hurt the recipient. The bully uses others to inflict pain by spreading rumors. Finally, social aggression damages the recipient's self-esteem or social status within a group by rumor spreading or social exclusion.

Although relational aggression can be as psychologically or emotionally destructive as the more direct and physical bullying behavior of boys, many school harassment policies focus on physical or direct violence and do not address relational aggression. In addition, female bullying is less likely to come to the attention of school personnel, even though students report that it is common. . . .

The Link Between Bullying and School Violence

Perhaps the most striking research to date has linked the effect of severe and repeated bullying to serious acts of violence. In 1999, the *Safe School Initiative*, a partnership between the U.S. Secret Service and the U.S. Department of Education, examined 37 incidents of targeted school shootings and school attacks involving 41 attackers, beginning with the first case in 1974. The Secret Service collected and analyzed all available information about each incident and conducted in-depth interviews with 10 of the shooters.

This research led to 10 key findings, one of which was that most of the attackers felt persecuted, bullied, threatened, attacked or injured by others prior to the incident. In several of these cases, the harassment the attackers endured was severe, long-standing, torturous and a significant factor in the attackers' decision to use violence. Witnesses in one case, for example, indicated that ". . . nearly every child in the school had at some point thrown the attacker against a locker, tripped him in the hall, held his head under water in the pool or thrown things at him." In fact, the Secret Service found that

Myths About Bullying

1. The Myth: Bullies suffer from insecurity and low self-esteem. They pick on others to make themselves feel more important.

The Research: Most bullies have average or above-average self-esteem. They "suffer" from aggressive temperaments, a lack of empathy, and poor parenting.

2. The Myth: Bullies are looking for attention. Ignore them and the bullying will stop.

The Research: Bullies are looking for control, and they rarely stop if their behavior is ignored. The level of bullying usually increases if the bullying is not addressed by adults.

3. The Myth: Boys will be boys.

The Research: Bullying is seldom outgrown; it's simply redirected. About 60 percent of boys identified as bullies in middle school commit at least one crime by the time they are 24.

4. The Myth: Kids can be cruel about differences.

The Research: Physical differences play only a very small role in bullying situations. Most victims are chosen because they are sensitive, anxious, and unable to retaliate.

5. The Myth: Victims of bullies need to learn to stand up for themselves and deal with the situation.

The Research: Victims of bullies are usually younger or physically weaker than their attackers. They also lack the social skills to develop supportive friendships. They cannot deal with the situation themselves.

"Sticks and Stones and Names Can Hurt You:
De-Myth-tifying the Classroom Bully!"
Education World, *July 11, 2000, updated May 11, 2005.*

more than half of the attackers cited revenge as a motive and more than three-quarters of attackers were known to hold a grievance against an individual or group of individuals before the attack. Released in May 2002, the *Safe School Initiative* final report concluded: "The prevalence of bullying found in this and other recent studies should strongly support ongoing efforts to reduce bullying in American schools."

Other Negative Effects of Bullying

Research has shown that long-term consequences are associated with bullying others and being bullied. Research conducted in 1993 indicates that children who are bullied often suffer from depression and low self-esteem well into adulthood. Moreover, the act of bullying can become a "gateway" to other negative behaviors in adolescence such as vandalism, shoplifting and drug use and to more serious crimes committed in adulthood. Sixty percent of males who were bullies in grades six through nine were convicted of at least one crime as adults, compared with 23 percent of males who did not engage in bullying others. Further, 40 percent of these former school bullies had three or more convictions by age 24, compared with 10 percent of their non-bullying peers.

The 1998 NICHHD [National Institute of Child Health and Human Development] survey found that students who were bullied reported more loneliness and more difficulty making friends than students who were not bullied. Further, those students who bullied others were more likely to have poor grades, smoke cigarettes and drink alcohol.

Finally, even though female bullying may not leave physical scars, the psychological effects can be carried into adulthood. Because girls are socialized to be nurturing caretakers and to value relationships, these connections are very important to them. As a result, fear of isolation and solitude can be severely damaging and destructive to girls.

Because students' reactions to bullying are influenced by a complex set of social and psychological factors, there is no formula for predicting when victims of bullying will respond with violence. Nevertheless, a great deal of research during the last two decades has identified personal characteristics and environmental conditions that, taken alone or in combination, work to protect kids from engaging in violent and dangerous behavior or that put them at risk of engaging in such behavior. At the same time, although children with multiple risk factors are substantially more likely to participate in risky, dangerous or violent behavior, some children who fit these criteria will not do so. In short, school-based victimization fits into a larger puzzle of personal and environmental circumstances of which bullying is but one piece.

The Link Between Bullying and Suicide

Although the research is beginning to paint a clearer picture of the effects of both being a bully and being victimized by them, other outcomes remain more difficult to measure. We know, for example, that kids who are bullied often suffer from depression, low self-esteem and loneliness. We also know that more than half of the attackers involved in school attacks since 1974 had a history of feeling extremely depressed or desperate and that nearly 75 percent of them threatened to kill themselves, made suicidal gestures or actually attempted suicide before they attacked the school. Although an association between being bullied and the desire or attempt to commit suicide is present in individual cases, it is also true that other bullied kids do not [experience the same desire]. The decision to commit or attempt suicide often involves a number of contributing factors. Isolating any particular factor—such as being bullied—as the primary cause often proves impossible scientifically unless compelling evidence—such as a note or post-attempt interview—warrants that conclusion. It is fair to say, however, that poor mental health is a consequence of being constantly belittled and harassed and that some children may be driven to end this victimization in extreme ways while others prove more resilient.

The Link Between Bullying and Academic Achievement

The research also is unclear about the effect(s) of bullying on academic achievement. Research has shown that kids who bully others are more likely to engage in a number of negative activities, to have poorer grades and to drop out of school at a higher rate than their peers. Again, because many factors both inside and outside school may be involved, the relationship is associational rather than causal. In other words, although bullies as a group share many of the same characteristics, it is not clear that having lower grades is caused by bullying others any more than bullying others is caused by receiving lower grades.

Research also has shown that children who are repeatedly bullied fear going to school or refuse to do so and have difficulty concentrating while in school. Although it seems unlikely that an ideal learning environment exists for students who are feeling alone, depressed, scared or desperate, the research has yet to answer why some bullied students struggle academically and others do not. . . .

As is the case with intervention in most negative human behavior, tackling the schoolyard bully is no easy task. Made complex at the outset by difficulties in defining exactly what bullying is, eliminating this behavior calls for a number of key participants to act together to create the right combination of sound policy, awareness of the problem, appropriate sanctions, successful prevention and intervention, data collection, evaluation and a fair amount of patience with the process. As state legislatures continue to address bullying, harassment and intimidation in schools, a number of tools will likely become available. What is known about bullying will continue to expand exponentially as more research is conducted, and evaluation of programs that work show positive outcomes. Reporting mechanisms will improve. Evaluation instruments to measure the extent of bullying or the outcomes of intervention will be refined and made available for use by others. States that choose to address bullying legislatively in the years to come will benefit from the experiences—positive or negative—of the states that currently are enacting anti-bullying policy. Although bullying may be only one piece of the complicated puzzle that is school violence, its elimination moves schools one step closer to being safe and productive places to learn for everyone inside the schoolhouse gate.

> *"In an adolescent whose growth and development are not yet complete, the medical consequences of eating disorders can be long lasting and irreversible."*

Eating Disorders Put Teens at Risk

B. Timothy Walsh and V.L. Cameron

B. Timothy Walsh and V.L. Cameron explain in the following viewpoint the serious risks for teens (girls as well as boys) with eating disorders. According to the authors, anorexia nervosa—one of the deadliest psychiatric disorders—leads to malnutrition, which in turn causes severe health complications including dangerously low blood pressure, deterioration of the heart and cardiovascular system, low white and red blood cell counts, seizures, and loss of bone development. B. Timothy Walsh is a medical doctor who founded the Eating Disorders Research Unit at the New York State Psychiatric Institute; V.L. Cameron is a freelance writer based in New York City.

As you read, consider the following questions:

1. According to the authors, at what phase in life does anorexia nervosa normally begin?
2. What definition do the authors give for the word "anorexia"?
3. Is the delay in bone development associated with anorexia nervosa more likely to occur in adolescent boys or girls, according to Walsh and Cameron?

When Chelsey started skipping meals and isolating herself from family and friends, her parents began to worry. "As a young girl, she was always so outgoing," her mother Donna says. "She had lots of friends and was involved in all kinds of social activities. She was also high-achieving and a perfectionist. Everything had to be done just so and if something wasn't done exactly the way she thought it should be, she'd become distressed and do it over and over again until she got it right. This perfectionistic attitude spilled over into her drive to be thin. When my husband and I finally told her she needed to stop dieting, she became angry and defensive with us for interfering in her life. That really took us by surprise because she'd never spoken to us that way before. We later found out that she didn't just want to be thin, she wanted to be thinner than everyone else."

Valerie noticed similar changes in her daughter Audra. "She became very withdrawn and secretive. She started acting as though there was some inner force driving her to keep moving and stay busy. She suddenly became very preoccupied and had a short attention span. As her physical condition deteriorated, she also became extremely short-tempered and her thinking was irrational at times. When her weight reached the critical stage, she even became violent."

Diane's first clue that something was wrong with Megan came when her daughter returned home after her first year away at college. "She was extremely thin, always cold, and looked unhealthy," Diane recalls. "Plus her relationship to food had completely changed. Before, she'd always loved food, she had celebrated it, but all that changed after she came back from school and it was clear she was seeing food in a different way. She suddenly agonized over what she could or couldn't eat, and grocery shopping turned into an exhausting ordeal because she had to calculate every calorie and fat gram. If the total amounted to more than she was willing to allow herself, she'd put the food back rather than adding it to the cart. Her healthy relationship with food had changed to an unhealthy one and trying to get her to eat anything became a nightmare."

Chelsey, Audra, and Megan were all exhibiting signs and symptoms of anorexia nervosa, a complex mental disorder that can cause a person to literally "waste away" due to an intense fear of being fat. Even when at a dangerously low weight, a teen can refer to herself as a "fat cow" because the disease distorts how people think about themselves.

Anorexia nervosa normally begins around the onset of puberty, and full-blown cases occur in about one in every 200 adolescents, with 90% to 95% of those teenagers being girls. Anorexia nervosa is one of the deadliest psychiatric disorders, with a mortality rate estimated at 0.56% per year, or approximately 5.6% per decade. That statistic is approximately 12 times higher than the annual death rate due to all causes of death among females between the ages 15 to 24 in the general population. . . .

By itself, the term *anorexia* actually means "loss of appetite." Virtually everyone has experienced anorexia: for example, "stomach flu" and a number of medications, like some types of chemotherapy drugs, can produce an aversion to food and cause weight loss. Those with the mental disorder "anorexia nervosa," however, do not have an aversion to food. In fact, they are almost always hungry and think about food constantly even as the disorder impels them to deny their bodies the fuel needed to function properly. This denial of the normal desire for food can even include going to great lengths to "protect" the disease, such as avoiding social occasions involving meals, trying to hide severe weight loss by wearing baggy clothes, or lying to family and friends about what they are or aren't eating.

"It's hard to believe that your own kid would lie right to your face," Diane says, "especially if they've never done it before. So when they say they had a big lunch or ate dinner with a friend, you believe them. There's nothing to tell you you shouldn't. I mean, who wants to think their daughter is not only a liar but is purposely trying to starve herself to death?"

While many children in the throes of anorexia nervosa do wind up actually starving themselves to a critical point physically, few set out with such a mission in mind. The disease can often take hold because they start out feeling betrayed by their changing bodies. With the onset of puberty, a girl suddenly has to deal with a figure that is becoming round and curvy—with growing breasts, hips, buttocks, and thighs— which can make her feel extremely self-conscious and even distressed. Likewise, an adolescent boy who grows wider instead of taller might be the object of ridicule from his peers because his "baby fat" makes him look too much like "a girl." In our culture, a remarkably high percentage of both boys and girls are unhappy with their appearance. According to one study of sixth to eighth graders, 26% of girls and 22% of boys believed they were significantly overweight, and even higher fractions of girls and boys were trying to lose weight. The dissatisfaction with physical appearance suggested by such statistics, along with the mental and physical changes that accompany the onset of puberty, can trigger all kinds of disordered-eating behaviors in sensitive children who define their self-worth by how they look.

Additionally, when some kids do go on a diet and lose weight, they can become so intoxicated with praise from friends or relatives (e.g., "Wow, you look great!" or "Man, that diet really worked, didn't it?") that they might think, "Well, if you think I look good now, just wait and see how good I look after I lose another ten pounds." Unfortunately, the more one becomes burdened with the drive to be thin or to maintain thinness, the more it can become an obsession. One adolescent even described herself as a "soldier" in the fight not to succumb to the enemy (hunger), with every second, every minute, and every hour of her life being driven by the need to win the "war" waged between her body and her need to control it.

Public awareness about anorexia nervosa has increased dramatically in the last few decades, in part because of the media's focus on celebrities with eating disorders. One of the earliest examples occurred in 1983, when Grammy Award–winning pop singer Karen Carpenter died of heart failure at the age of 32 as a result of the long-term effects of self-starvation, self-induced vomiting, and laxative abuse.

"At the time I was completely shocked," says a mother whose daughter died of an eating disorder some 15 years later. "How could someone as rich and famous as Karen Carpenter die at such a young age simply because she'd gone on a diet? Back then we really didn't understand the difference between just dieting and having an eating disorder. Her death made headlines all over the country, but they only said she'd died because her heart gave out, making us think that it was a biological or genetic problem. It wasn't until years later—when my own daughter was diagnosed—that I was finally able to learn more about how insidious eating disorders really are.". . .

Eating disorders are associated with serious medical complications and can be fatal. Most of the complications result from malnutrition or occur as a result of unhealthy weight-control behaviors, like vomiting. Even adolescents who do not meet full criteria for anorexia nervosa or bulimia nervosa but have symptoms of eating disorders may be at risk of developing these complications. Serious though they can be, most of the complications are reversible with nutritional rehabilitation and symptomatic improvement. However, in an adolescent whose growth and development are not yet complete, the medical consequences of eating disorders can be long lasting and irreversible. Particularly worrisome complications for adolescents include growth retardation, pubertal delay or arrest, and impaired acquisition of bone mass.

Medical Complications of Anorexia Nervosa

The most notable medical complications of anorexia nervosa result from malnutrition. Muscle wastes, cheeks are sunken, and bones protrude through the skin, which itself may be pale, dry, and yellow in color. Body temperature is usually low, and the individual's hands and feet may be cold and blue; he or she will often need multiple layers of clothing to keep warm. Fine downy hair (lanugo) may be present over the arms, back, and face. Scalp hair is dry, listless, and brittle, and there may be evidence of hair loss. Resting pulse and blood pressure are both low—for example, the pulse may be as low as 30 to 40 beats per minute, in contrast to the normal average of between 60 and 100 beats per minute—and changes in both pulse and blood pressure, such as what occurs when the person stands up, may cause dizziness or fainting.

Malnutrition can lead to life-threatening deterioration in the functioning of the heart and cardiovascular system. The effects of malnutrition are often aggravated by imbalances of electrolytes, which are minerals like sodium and potassium needed to maintain physical functions, such as heart rhythm, muscle contraction, and brain function. An electrolyte imbalance is more likely to occur in those who are vomiting or abusing laxatives or diuretics. Individuals who drink excessive amounts of water, either to defray hunger or to falsely elevate

Eating Disorders Do Not Discriminate

One of the biggest misconceptions about the prevalence of eating disorders is that they affect only "white girls." However, as the Office on Women's Health (OWH) points out, an increasing number of girls and boys from all ethnic and racial groups are suffering from eating disorders, although their cases can go unreported "due to the lack of studies that include representatives from these groups." As Drs. Marian Fitzgibbon and Melinda Stolley speculate in *Minority Women: The Untold Story*, the reason for the exclusion of minorities in early research on eating disorders was due to most studies only being conducted on college campuses or in hospital clinics. They state, "For reasons related to economics, access to care, and cultural attitudes toward psychological treatment, middle-class white females were the ones seeking treatment and thus became the subjects of research." Also, the OWH surmises that girls of different ethnic and cultural groups may not seek treatment because of "difficulty in locating culturally sensitive treatment centers."

B. Timothy Walsh and V.L. Cameron,
If Your Adolescent Has an Eating Disorder:
An Essential Resource for Parents. *New York:
Oxford University Press, 2005 Copyright © 2005
Oxford University Press, Inc. Reproduced
by permission of Oxford University Press, Inc.*

body weight before a medical visit, risk low sodium levels (hyponatremia) as well as seizures, coma, and death caused by "water intoxication."

Medical complications such as congestive heart failure can occur during the early phases of refeeding. Bloating and constipation are frequent complaints of patients with anorexia nervosa, indicating delayed gastric emptying and decreased intestinal functioning. Malnutrition also causes the metabolism to slow down, requiring fewer calories to function. Suppression of the bone marrow often occurs, resulting in low white blood cell, red blood cell, and platelet counts. Despite the low white blood cell count, there does not appear to be an increased risk of infection. The major neurological complications of eating disorders are seizures and cerebral atrophy (a reduction in the size of the brain), as well as impairment of attention, concentration, and memory.

The occurrence of anorexia nervosa prior to the completion of an individual's growth interferes with bone development, and some adolescents may never reach their full height. The delay in bone growth is more likely to occur in adolescent boys than in girls because boys grow, on average, for two years longer than girls, whose growth is almost complete by their first menstruation (usually around age 12). In both boys and girls, anorexia nervosa disrupts the hormonal changes that are a normal part of puberty. For example, as we mentioned previously, loss of menstruation, or amenorrhea, is a cardinal feature of anorexia nervosa among girls. Pituitary and ovarian hormones controlling menstruation are all low, and the uterus and ovaries shrink in size. If weight is restored and the girl's menstrual periods resume, however, the ability to conceive should be normal.

A serious side effect of prolonged amenorrhea and a low estrogen state is osteopenia, a substantial reduction in bone mass. It is related to poor nutrition, low body weight, estrogen deficiency, and high levels of cortisol (a hormone released by the adrenal glands that is responsible for many of the physiological effects of stress) in the blood stream. The reduction in bone density in females with anorexia nervosa is more severe than it is in those with other conditions associated with amenorrhea and a low estrogen state, suggesting that, in addition to estrogen deficiency, nutritional factors play an important role.

Adolescence is a critical time for bone mass acquisition. Whether or not a young woman will develop osteoporosis in later life depends not only on the rate of bone loss in adulthood, but also on the amount of bone present at skeletal maturity, often referred to as "peak bone mass." Many studies have shown that peak bone mass is achieved toward the end of the second decade of life. A woman who develops anorexia nervosa during adolescence may not reach a normal peak bone mass, placing her at increased risk of developing fractures. This risk may persist for years after recovery from the disorder.

It must also be reiterated that anorexia nervosa has one of the highest mortality rates among psychiatric disorders. The most common causes of death among patients struggling with the disorder are the effects of starvation and suicide. The suicide rate among women with anorexia nervosa is approximately 50 times higher than for women of a similar age in the general population.

> *"People need to hear from their local communities that bullying based on sexual orientation is a problem that really needs to be addressed."*

Gay Teens Are at Risk

Matthew S. Robinson

Matthew S. Robinson reveals in the following viewpoint the harassment and bullying that gay teens encounter at their schools. A Harris Interactive survey indicated that almost 38 percent of students polled reported that they had been "frequently or often" harassed at school, and 25 percent said they had been physically harassed because of their sexual identity. Robinson points out that quality supportive programs and legislation are overdue in providing a safe, nonthreatening environment for gay students. Matthew S. Robinson is a journalist and early-childhood educator from Boston.

As you read, consider the following questions:

1. According to a Gay, Lesbian, and Straight Education Network (GLSEN) survey as cited in the viewpoint,

what is the main reason that lesbian, gay, bisexual, and transgender (LGBT) students skip school and decide not to pursue postsecondary education?

2. What are the two states mentioned in the viewpoint that have established anti-bullying policies that specifically mention sexual orientation?

3. In those states that have established policies against acts of harassment based on sexual orientation, has the rate of bullying decreased, according to GLSEN?

Some of us—labeled too short, too heavy, not cool, or overly nerdy—know what it is to be teased or bullied at school. Some derision can be shrugged off, but when harassment becomes the defining element of academic life, it is essential to have somewhere to turn or someone to rely on.

For Elizabeth, a bisexual teen from Maryland who wishes to remain anonymous, life at school was misery. "My freshman year, only once did a teacher ever stop someone saying, 'That's so gay!'" she recalls. "No one ever stopped the kids." Not knowing how or where to find help, Elizabeth became discouraged. "I didn't talk to as many people as I might have," she admits, "because I didn't want to get to know somebody who wouldn't accept me if I were gay."

Harassment Due to Sexual Identity

In a recent national survey of more than 3,400 gay and straight students and 1,000 educators, 65 percent reported verbal abuse or physical assaults rooted in homophobia and prejudice in the last year. Commissioned by the Gay, Lesbian and Straight Education Network (GLSEN), the Harris Interactive Survey also indicated that 84 percent of those surveyed reported hearing derogatory remarks such as "faggot" or "dyke" at school, and nearly 70 percent reported hearing "gay" used in a derogatory manner.

In addition, almost 38 percent of students polled said that they had "frequently or often" been subjected to harassment

at school and one-fourth said they had been physically harassed because of their sexual identity.

"This is not a fringe issue that affects a few kids," says
Kevin Jennings, founder and executive director of GLSEN, a
national organization for gay and straight students as well as
supporters and school administrators. "It is a problem at the
center of bullying and harassment in schools." Reg Weaver,
president of the National Education Association (NEA), says
on the topic, "It is absolutely critical that the school environment is conducive to learning. To the extent that does not
happen, we need to take steps to try to ensure that for all
kids."

Though school presents challenges to all students, lesbian,
gay, bisexual, and transgender [LGBT] students face many
pressures and problems their fellow students do not. As a result, the GLSEN survey found, the LGBT students are five
times more likely to skip school and are only half as likely to
pursue postsecondary education, mainly because, like Elizabeth, they feel alienated and unsafe.

The survey also notes that the average grade-point average
for LGBT students who were harassed was half a grade lower
than that of other LGBT students (2.6 versus 3.1). In fact,
many simply do not attend as many classes even when they
are enrolled. "There are a whole range of bad outcomes edu-
cationally," Jennings says. "The climate is a direct result of the
failure of policy makers to deal with it."

Attempts at Organizing Support Groups

GLSEN and its partner programs are working hard to keep
this issue in the public eye and on state and federal political
agendas. Meanwhile, many students are seeking to create gay-
straight alliances and other organizations at their schools to
offer support and camaraderie to LGBT students. "These alli-

Victimization of LGBT Youth

LGBT youth face the threat of victimization everywhere: at home, at school, at their jobs, and, for those who are out-of-home, at shelters and on the streets. According to the National Runaway Switchboard, LGBT homeless youth are seven times more likely than their heterosexual peers to be victims of a crime. While some public safety agencies try to help this vulnerable population, others adopt a "blame the victim" approach, further decreasing the odds of victimized youth feeling safe reporting their experiences.

While there is a paucity of academic research about the experiences of LGBT youth who end up in the juvenile and criminal justice systems, preliminary evidence suggests that they are disproportionately the victims of harassment and violence, including rape. For example, respondents in one small study reported that lesbians and bisexual girls are overrepresented in the juvenile justice system and that they are forced to live among a population of inmates who are violently homophobic. Gay male youth in the system are also emotionally, physically and sexually assaulted by staff and inmates. One respondent in a study of the legal rights of young people in state custody reported that staff members think that "[if] a youth is gay, they want to have sex with all the other boys, so they did not protect me from unwanted sexual advances."

Nicholas Ray,
"Lesbian, Gay, Bisexual and Transgender Youth:
An Epidemic of Homelessness," The National
Gay and Lesbian Task Force, 2006. www.theTaskForce.org.

ances can be a powerful force for change in schools, as well as providing a safe place for people of all sexual orientations," Elizabeth says.

Unfortunately, many of these groups face problems of their own. "My freshman year, I joined my school's rapidly deteriorating Rainbow Alliance," she adds, noting that her school would not allow this organization to be called a "gay-straight alliance." "Pretty soon, I was the only one showing up to meetings."

In Bardstown, Kentucky, about an hour south of Louisville, Nelson County High School student Leslie Bartley also has been having difficulty organizing an alliance. "It is really hard finding a teacher sponsor, because there is apparently a negative image," she says. Another reason Bartley cites for the lack of faculty support is that only about thirty of the school's 1,300 students identify as LGBT.

Even so, Bartley is determined to make a difference. "I am going to try to start a day of action and talk to teachers to work to raise awareness," says Bartley, who is also a member of GLSEN's Jump-Start team, a national union of high-school-age student supporters that works to end discrimination against LGBT students. "I am the student council secretary and a good student, so hopefully I can talk to people and help out."

Though some of these student groups deteriorate on their own, others are subject to outside influences. In Virginia, there has been an effort to pass commonwealth-wide legislation that would require students to obtain parental permission to join any extracurricular groups, including LGBT organizations. "This policy discriminates against gay-straight alliances," says Dyana Mason, executive director of Equality Virginia (EV). "It is a thinly veiled attempt to encourage school boards who do not understand the nature of gay-straight alliances."

So far [February 2008], the bills have not passed the Virginia legislature, but one has been proposed each of the last three years. Each year, says EV political-committee chair David Lampo, the wording of the measure becomes more sophisticated. "Now, they talk about 'parental choice,'" he notes. "It is no longer an outright prohibition or requirement for permission slips."

This year's [2008] bill, Lampo says, proposed an opt-in policy in which students had to get permission to join any extracurricular activity. "It was a much better bill from the perspective of its opponents," he adds, "because it mandated that every district have its own policy." But the potential complications of keeping track of a number of policies and their enforcement put off school administrators, and the bill was again stalled in the state's education committee.

Political Involvement

In nine other states, antibullying policies have been established that specifically mention sexual orientation. In these states, which include California, New Jersey, Washington, and Wisconsin, rates of bullying, including acts of harassment based on sexual orientation, are 25 percent lower. "They send a message as to what a school will and will not accept," GLSEN's Kevin Jennings suggests.

Tyler, a recent high school graduate in Iowa, went to work with the Iowa Safe School Task Force, and attended a conference on LGBT issues convened by Governor Chet Culver. "The fact that the governor organized this shows that there are political figures who are also tired of the bullying," Tyler says.

Another supportive politician is Michigan state senator Glenn S. Anderson. After surveying fifty-six school districts across the state and finding many to be lacking any kind of harassment protections, Anderson introduced a measure that would require every school to have at least a basic form of bullying policy that covers race, religion, color, age, sex, and actual or perceived sexual orientation.

"No matter where they attend school, every child has the right to have a safe, nonthreatening environment," Anderson says. Though forty-six co-sponsors have endorsed Anderson's bill and the state board of education, the state police, and Michigan governor Jennifer Granholm support it, legislative priorities have prevented its passing thus far.

Other state legislatures appear to be waking up to this aspect of the age-old bullying issue, but many of them need reminding and support, especially when facing off against other legislative priorities or against colleagues who do not want, or don't see a need for, LGBT students to have any special protections or rights. "I need help," Anderson admits. "People need to hear from their local communities that bullying based on sexual orientation is a problem that really needs to be addressed."

That is where organizations like the Triangle Foundation come in. Since 1991, Triangle has supported the LGBT community in Michigan and elsewhere. Now the group is working on passing policies that specifically protect LGBT students. "We're trying to pass antibullying legislation that protects all kids, including LGBT youth," says Sean Kosofsky, the foundation's director of policy. By promoting a more universal policy, he suggests, the bill, which recently passed in the state House of Representatives, is more likely to have success in the state Senate.

Kevin Jennings is disappointed with the generic bullying policies being pursued in states such as Michigan and believes that they don't have enough impact for LGBT students. Even so, many legislators and educators agree that general policies are better than no policies, and they continue to push for them in the hope that they will lead to more understanding and better treatment of LGBT students.

"Whenever we see that these policies are nonexistent, we try to work with the appropriate folks," says the NEA's Reg Weaver. "It is not where we would like it to be, but hopefully it is better than where it was."

Periodical Bibliography

The following articles have been selected to supplement the diverse views presented in this chapter.

Associated Press — "Scientists Say Teen Brain, Still Maturing, Key to Behavior," *Daily Herald*, December 2, 2007.

Salynn Boyles — "Teens Are Hardwired for Risky Behavior," *WebMD Medical News*, April 13, 2007.

Maria R. T. deGuzman — "Friendships, Peer Influence, and Peer Pressure During the Teen Years," *NebGuide*, University of Nebraska, August 2007.

Paul Grondahl — "There's Nothing Funny About Being Fat," *San Diego Union Tribune*, January 22, 2008.

Lawrence Jones — "Popular Culture Driving Teen Violence, Say Christians," *The Christian Post*, December 12, 2007.

Christopher Maag — "Technology Leaves Kids with Nowhere to Hide from Cyberbullying," *San Diego Union Tribune*, December 29, 2007.

Jen Pearl — "Gay Youths More at Risk of Homelessness," StreetSense.org, June 2006.

Society for Neuroscience — "Why Teens Are Such Impulsive Risk-Takers," *Science Daily*, November 8, 2007.

Students Against Destructive Decisions (SADD) — "Teens and Sleep: What You Should Know," SADD.org, Spring 2004.

Laurie Udesky — "Ills & Conditions: Depression and Violence in Teens," *Caremark Health Resources*, July 31, 2006.

Melody Warnick — "Less-Stressed Kids: 10 Ways To Help Your Child Chill Out," *Better Homes and Gardens*, February 2008.

OPPOSING
VIEWPOINTS®
SERIES

CHAPTER 2

Can Adverse Consequences of Teenage Sex and Pregnancy Be Reduced?

Chapter Preface

One in four teenage girls in the United States has a sexually transmitted disease (STD). That statistic was released on March 11, 2008, by researchers from the U.S. Centers for Disease Control and Prevention (CDC) as part of the agency's national STD Prevention Conference in Chicago. The CDC findings, which were based on a national health study using survey data, translates to an estimated 3.2 million adolescent girls nationwide infected with at least one of the four most common STDs—human papillomavirus (HPV), chlamydia, trichomoniasis, and herpes. Other STDs, such as syphilis, gonorrhea, and HIV, were not included in the study. While most health experts were alarmed and disappointed at the results of the study, some were not surprised. Daryl Lynch, a physician in the Teen Clinic of Children's Mercy Hospital in Kansas City, Missouri, remarked, "We have historically seen lots and lots of STDs among teens in Kansas City. It's a very sexually active, sexually promiscuous crowd that doesn't practice safe sex. And therein lies the problem."

Although teenage boys also carry sexually transmitted diseases, the researchers focused on females because of their higher risk for severe and life-threatening consequences. For example, HPV—which was found to be the most common STD among teenage girls—can cause cervical cancer and genital warts, and often has no physical symptoms. Chlamydia—which was found to be the second most common infection—can cause pelvic inflammatory disease and, if left untreated, infertility. Chlamydia also often has no symptoms. Trichomoniasis is associated with abnormal discharge and painful urination, and genital herpes causes blisters and is not curable.

Given the widespread prevalence of these potentially dangerous sexually transmitted diseases among adolescent girls, the critical question becomes: what can be done to lower the rate? Experts disagree on the answer. Moira Gaul, Family Research Council's director of women's health, declaired, "Only a risk-avoidance or sexual abstinence-until-marriage strategy will be effective in helping to reverse the current STD epidemic." But Cecile Richards of Planned Parenthood Federation of America said the study shows that "the national policy of promoting abstinence-only programs is a 1.5 billion dollar failure and teenage girls are paying the real price." Others recommend a middle ground. Ellen Kruger, an obstetrician-gynecologist at Ochsner Medical Center in New Orleans, said, "Teens need to hear the dual message that STDs can be prevented by abstinence and condoms." Dr. Elizabeth Alderman, adolescent medicine specialist at Montefiore Medical Center's Children's Hospital in New York, agrees. "To talk about abstinence is not a bad thing," she said. "But teen girls—and boys, too—need to be informed about how to protect themselves if they do have sex."

On the medical side, the CDC recommends better promotion of prevention and screening practices. In particular, parents could provide their daughters with the HPV vaccine Gardasil to reduce the risk of cervical cancer. And because many STDs start out as infections with no symptoms, regular screening is vital so that antibiotic treatment can be initiated.

The spread of STDs is just one of many issues in the discussion about teenage sexual activity. The authors in the following chapter debate ways to mitigate other negative consequences of teen sex.

> "Teenagers in abstinence-education pro-
> grams are significantly less likely to be
> sexually active than their peers."

Abstinence Sex Education Reduces Teen Sexual Activity

Emma Elliott

*Emma Elliott defends abstinence-only sex education in the fol-
lowing viewpoint against several claims made by proponents of
comprehensive "safe sex" education programs. The author contends that abstinence sex education is indeed effective in deterring teenage sexual activity and that abstinence is the only way
to prevent teenage pregnancy and sexually transmitted diseases.
She further contends that "safe sex" education programs give
teens incorrect information that leads to a false sense of security.
Emma Elliott wrote this viewpoint for Concerned Women for
America, the nation's largest public policy women's organization
dedicated to promoting biblical values.*

As you read, consider the following questions:

1. According to Emma Elliott, how many teens every day
   become infected with a sexually transmitted disease?

Emma Elliott, "What Your Teacher Didn't Tell You About Abstinence," Concerned
Women for America, cwfa.org, December 2005. Reproduced by permission.

2. As stated in the viewpoint, what factor have major studies found to be causing the decline in pregnancies and abortions?

3. According to the author, what has the U.S. Department of Health and Human Services reported in relation to condom use and the prevention of sexually transmitted diseases?

From the media to the classroom, teens today are constantly being inundated with "safe sex" claims. They will become sexually active anyway, the thinking goes, so let's teach them how to do it "safely"—that is, with contraception. Teenagers are told it is fine to practice "safe sex" and abstinence is given short shrift. But that lie could ultimately destroy them.

Claim #1: Abstinence education doesn't work.

Proponents of "safe sex" education insist that abstinence education fails to deter teenage sexual activity. However, no fewer than 10 studies have shown that teenagers in abstinence-education programs are significantly less likely to be sexually active than their peers. Four of these studies were published in peer-reviewed journals. One of them showed that Best Friends, a program for girls aimed at reducing high-risk behavior such as sexual activity and drug use, produced an 80 percent reduction in the likelihood its participants would have sex.

Claim #2: Abstinence education increases pregnancy and the rate of sexually transmitted diseases [STDs].

One of the most insidious lies says that abstinence education denies teenagers "vital" information on contraceptives. The Web site of NARAL Pro-Choice America presents the story of "Katie" who tells how Miss America Heather Whitestone came to her school to talk about abstinence. Katie describes Whitestone's discussion of the risk of condom failure and then says, "A couple of months later the first girl got pregnant. The second girl got pregnant a few weeks later." Katie herself became pregnant and had an abortion.

NARAL, in its twisted reality, blames Miss America for telling the truth about condoms, rather than sexual activity, for these pregnancies. But studies that purport to show that abstinence education is the problem have been exposed as junk science. "Safe sex" has been around for years. Yet, more than 8,000 teens become infected with a sexually transmitted disease *every day*, and about 40 percent of sexually active teens eventually become pregnant out-of-wedlock. Abstinence is the only sure way to combat these troubling statistics.

Claim #3: Condoms and other contraceptives are causing the recent decline in teen pregnancies.

Thankfully, the teen pregnancy rate dropped 28 percent between 1990 and 2000. At the same time, abortions for 15- to 19-year-olds decreased 43 percent from 1988 to 2000. Proponents of "safe sex" argue that these declines prove their message is working. However, this is not reasonable when one considers the failure rates of condoms and contraceptives. Major studies have shown that less sex by teenagers, not increased use of condoms and contraceptives, is causing this. When abstinence is taught, the message gets through powerfully.

Claim #4: Condoms and contraceptives are nearly foolproof.

Perhaps the greatest lie told by "safe sex" proponents is that there even is such a thing as "safe sex." This could cost teenagers their lives. While sexually active characters on television programs virtually never contract STDs, millions of real teenagers will this year. Reports from the U.S. Department of Health and Human Services indicate that condoms, at best, *sometimes* prevent the transmission of sexually transmitted diseases including HIV, gonorrhea, chlamydia, syphilis, cancroids, trichomoniasis, genital herpes and human papillomavirus. Other contraceptives provide *no* protection from STDs. Condoms have an estimated 15 percent failure rate in pre-

Teens and Parents Favor Abstinence

There is strong and widespread support of teaching sexual abstinence to American teens. Over 90 percent of parents, at a minimum, want teens to be taught to abstain from sexual activity until they have at least finished high school. (Some 84 percent of parents favor teaching a stronger standard: abstinence until a couple is married or close to marriage.) Teens themselves also favor abstinence education: over 90 percent agree that teens should be taught to abstain from sex until they have at least finished high school.

Robert Rector and Kirk A. Johnson,
"Teenage Sexual Abstinence and Academic Achievement,"
October 27, 2005. The Heritage Foundation.

venting pregnancy. The only truly "safe" option is abstinence until marriage and faithfulness thereafter.

Claim #5: Abstinence education is everywhere.

Those who teach "safe sex" like to pretend that abstinence education is the norm in public schools. Organizations like Planned Parenthood and politicians like Rep. Henry Waxman (D-California) focus primarily on President [George W.] Bush's recent increases in funding for abstinence education. This is unrealistic. President Bush called for $250 million to be spent on abstinence education in 2005; Congress approved only $168 million. On the other hand, $653 million was spent on condom-based sex education. This imbalance must change for abstinence education to fulfill its potential.

Claim #6: "Abstinence-plus" education is better.

Proponents of "safe sex" pretend there is middle ground in what they euphemistically call "comprehensive" sex education or "abstinence-plus." They want to sabotage the authentic abstinence message by including instruction in condom and contraception use. But that's a mixed message. We don't tell children not to do drugs and then give them clean syringes in case they do. We don't tell them not to smoke and then give them low-tar cigarettes because those are the least harmful. We don't do those things because they undermine the point we are trying to make. Another strike against so-called "abstinence-plus" education is that it contains very little abstinence. The Heritage Foundation examined nine different curricula and found that, in a total of 942 pages, not one single sentence urged students to abstain from sexual activity.

Claim #7 "Everybody's doing it."

Many teens today have the impression that everyone their age is sexually active. However, research reports that in 2003 fully 53 percent of high school students reported never having had sex. This is up from 46 percent in 1991. This fact needs to be promoted—and abstinent teenagers ought to be supported and encouraged, not ridiculed or ignored.

Claim #8: It's normal and healthy for teenagers to have sex.

Nothing could be further from the truth. The vast majority of teenagers, 72 percent of girls and 55 percent of boys, admit regret over early sexual activity. The vast majority of teenage pregnancies occur unintentionally and outside of marriage. Of those who carry their babies to term, only one-third will complete high school and 80 percent will begin to rely on government welfare within five years. Sexually active girls are three times more likely to be depressed and three times more likely to commit suicide than girls who are abstinent. Sexually active boys are twice as likely to be depressed and eight times more likely to commit suicide than boys who are abstinent. Sexual activity can be extremely harmful to teenagers.

"Today, sadly, there are far too many teens with broken hearts and incurable diseases." writes Dr. Janice Crouse of the Beverly LaHaye Institute, "because adults are unwilling to state categorically that sex is meant exclusively for marriage."

> "I am completely against abstinence-only sex ed programs for three reasons: there is no evidence at all that they work; common sense says they have no chance of working; and it is not clear that ethically they send the right message to young people."

Abstinence Sex Education Does Not Reduce Teen Sexual Activity

Arthur Caplan

In the following viewpoint, Arthur Caplan maintains that abstinence-only sex education causes more harm than good. Research has shown that teens who pledged virginity until marriage as part of abstinence-only sex education contracted sexually transmitted diseases at rates similar to other teens, but were less likely to use contraception. The author asserts that most teenagers will engage in sexual activity; therefore, it only makes sense that they should be informed about contraception and the

Arthur Caplan, "Abstinence-Only Sex Ed Defies Common Sense: Education Policy Spreads Ignorance, Sends Confusing Message to Teens," MSNBC.com, October 13, 2005. © 2008 MSNBC Interactive. Republished with permission of MSNBC.com, conveyed through Copyright Clearance Center, Inc.

facts regarding sexually transmitted diseases. Arthur Caplan is director of the Center for Bioethics at the University of Pennsylvania.

As you read, consider the following questions:

1. According to recent surveys as stated in the viewpoint, what percent of U.S. teens have had sexual intercourse before reaching the age of eighteen?
2. According to the viewpoint, have abstinence-only sex education programs been successful in reducing sexual activity?
3. Do teenagers feel the abstinence message has more impact when promoted at schools than it does when it comes from parents, according to Caplan?

There may be a sillier strategy for dealing with sex among teens than promoting the choice of "abstinence-only-until-marriage," but I am not quite sure what it is. Not only is such an approach contradicted by everything that medicine and science know about teens and sex, but it flies directly in the face of everything all ordinary Americans know about teens and sex.

Recent surveys show that 70 percent of U.S. teens have engaged in oral sex by the time they reach 18, and more than 45 percent have had intercourse at least once. More than 70 percent of young women and 80 percent of young men approve of premarital sex, according to a study published recently in the *Review of General Psychology*.

In addition, studies show sexually transmitted diseases [STDs] are spreading at an alarming rate among young people. The Centers for Disease Control and Prevention reports that nearly half of the nation's new cases of STDs each year occur among adolescents and young adults. A recent study found that teens who took pledges of virginity as part of abstinence-only sex ed classes ultimately had STD rates similar to other young people and were less likely to use contraception or other forms of protection when they did become sexually active.

In short, the idea that teens will remain celibate until they marry—and that they don't need information about sex—says much more about the values and fantasies of the people who are promoting these policies than it does about teens.

Confusing Messages

So what should we teach our kids about sex? Most Americans want young people to be taught about sexuality as part of their junior high school and high school education, but there is almost no agreement on what the content of sex education should be. Popular opinion ranges from telling kids to "just say no" to how to find a woman's "G-spot." And since sex brings out our sense of morality like almost no other subject, science and the facts about sexual behavior tend to get lost in a lot of finger-pointing and teeth-gnashing.

For instance, in North Dakota, sex education is encouraged but there are few guidelines about what should be taught. In South Carolina, state law severely restricts sex education. There can be no discussion of contraception except with reference to marriage, no discussion of abortion, and nothing said about homosexuality except with reference to preventing sexually transmitted diseases. And in Texas, at least since the days when George W. Bush was governor, sex ed classes almost exclusively espouse abstinence-only messages.

In contrast, Oregon, California and New Jersey mandate that if a school does teach about sex it must provide medically accurate information, and age-appropriate and respectful discussion of the diversity of relationships, including those involving people with disabilities.

Ineffective Results

I am completely against abstinence only sex ed programs for three reasons: there is no evidence at all that they work; com-

"Am I Glad to Get That Straightened Out Now, I Can Go Home and Explain It to My Dad," cartoon by Marty Bucella. CartoonStock.com.

mon sense says they have no chance of working; and it is not clear that ethically they send the right message to young people.

But under the [George W.] Bush administration, the federal government has planted itself firmly in the abstinence-only camp. More than a billion dollars have been spent to support these programs.

To make matters worse, the administration and Congress have played favorites with your tax money, with abstinence-only money going disproportionately to Arizona, Florida,

Georgia and Texas. In contrast, Vermont received the least amount of federal funding. Maybe the kids in Vermont cannot hear admonitions to remain chaste amidst the sound of falling snow?

Eleven states have tried to evaluate their abstinence-only programs and the results have been dismal. In Kansas, the evaluators stated that "no changes [were] noted in participants' actual or intended behavior." Evaluators of the Texas program found the same thing—no change in the number of students pledging to remain celibate until marriage. In fact, more students reported having had sex after taking an abstinence-only sex ed course than they did beforehand.

There is no evidence at all that telling kids not to fool around has any more impact when the message is promoted by schools than it does when parents say the same thing at home.

Sex and Common Sense

Which leads us to the world of sex and common sense. There are kids who are not going to have sex in junior high or high school. There are, according to what social scientists know about teens, not a lot of such kids but there are some. There are also some teens who are going to engage in homosexual acts and other non-standard forms of sexual contact. There are not a lot of these kids out there, according to what social scientists know, but there are some. An even smaller number of kids will, tragically, be forced to have sex by parents, relatives or rapists.

The fact is that a teen has a pretty good chance of getting involved in sex before graduating from high school and a small chance of being involved in something other than consensual male-female sexual intercourse. In addition to there being no evidence that abstinence-only sex ed works, there is no reason to believe that this form of sex education is even on the same planet as those it is intended to reach.

Attitudes of Parents

So what message is sent to teens when abstinence-only-until-marriage is portrayed as the only acceptable way to deal with sex?

When I went to child-parent meetings at my son's high school, parents of girls were frantic that the school reinforce the message that sexual intercourse was a bad choice. Parents of boys always seemed to me to be supportive but not nearly as frantic that this message be taught.

However, parents' attitudes seemed to change when these same kids went away to college or went off to get a job. A lot of these very same parents stopped preaching that sex before marriage was wrong. A fair number of them would whisper that sex before marriage might be a good idea, especially if the sex was with someone their son or daughter was thinking about marrying. Many of these parents had lived with someone before marrying and all of them who had done so had sex before marrying.

The message that sex must wait until marriage is not the right message to send to a young person. The people sending the message almost never lived up to it in their own lives and nothing turns a kid off like hypocrisy. Furthermore, most kids themselves just don't believe it.

And lastly, regardless of what someone's age is, it makes more sense to talk about maturity, love and mutual respect than to send an absolute message that sex is unacceptable outside marriage—a message that gets nullified the day a person graduates from high school.

Science and common sense, not wishful thinking and hypocrisy, should guide what we teach kids about sex.

> "Public policy has long protected the right of minors to receive contraceptive services confidentially. The same is not true for abortion, notwithstanding research suggesting that policies mandating parental involvement in either case present a significant threat to teenagers' health and well-being."

Teens Should Be Allowed an Abortion Without Parental Consent

Cynthia Dailard and Chinue Turner Richardson

In the following viewpoint, the authors discuss the public policy debates over parent involvement in reproductive health services, and whether teenagers should be allowed to obtain such services confidentially. The viewpoint contends the public policies that restore parental rights are potentially harmful to teenagers' health. Cynthia Dailard and Chinue Turner Richardson are authors for the Guttmacher Report on Public Policy.

Cynthia Dailard and Chinue Turner Richardson, "Teenagers' Access to Confidential Reproductive Health Services," *The Guttmacher Report on Public Policy*, The Guttmacher Institute, November 2005.

As you read, consider the following questions:

1. What is "Title X of the Public Health Service Act"?

2. According to the viewpoint, how many teenagers in states without a parental consent requirement say one or both parents knew about the abortion?

3. Why have lower federal courts held the New Hampshire statute unconstitutional?

The public policy debate over whether teenagers should be allowed to obtain reproductive health services confidentially or required to involve their parents dates back to the 1970s, when teen sexual activity became increasingly visible and teen pregnancy was first deemed a national social problem. Although teenagers did not initiate sexual activity any earlier over the course of that decade (according to groundbreaking surveys measuring levels of teenage sexual activity), the age of marriage was rising. Therefore, pregnancies that would have occurred to teenagers within marriage in previous years increasingly occurred before marriage. At the same time, pregnant teenagers became less likely to marry to "legitimize" their pregnancies and births, and more teens began to terminate their pregnancies following the national legalization of abortion in 1973.

Meanwhile, a growing body of research demonstrated that teenagers who gave birth had worse maternal and child health outcomes than did those who postponed childbearing, and that these young women were more likely to be poor and have reduced educational and workforce achievement. Reproductive health providers and others concerned about adolescent health and well-being increasingly turned their attention to ensuring that teenagers had the information and services they needed to avoid early and unwanted pregnancy. New laws and policies at the state and federal levels began to allow teenagers to consent to reproductive health services and to ensure that services would be delivered confidentially when requested. And in the late 1970s, the Supreme Court in successive decisions extended the constitutional right to privacy to a minor's decision to both obtain contraceptives and choose an abortion.

These developments, however, produced a political backlash among social and religious conservatives, who contended that the very availability of confidential reproductive health services promoted sexual promiscuity among teens, undermined parental authority and interfered with parent-child relationships. They argued, then and now, that state and federal law should enshrine parents' rights to control their children's upbringing, and they have worked consistently over the course of three decades to legislate parental control over teenagers' reproductive health care decisions.

Public Policy on Minors' Rights

Parents generally have the legal authority to make medical decisions on behalf of their minor children, on the basis that young people typically lack the maturity and judgment to make fully informed decisions before they reach the age of majority (18 in most states). Exceptions to this rule have long existed, such as when medical emergencies leave no time to obtain parental consent and in cases where a minor is "emancipated" by marriage or other circumstances and thus can legally make decisions on his or her own behalf. Furthermore, some state courts have adopted the so-called mature minor rule, under which a minor who is deemed sufficiently intelligent and mature to understand the nature and consequences of a proposed treatment may consent to medical treatment without consulting his or her parents or obtaining their permission.

On the basis of scientific findings dating back to the late 1970s that identified the premium that young people place on confidentiality, public policy has long reflected the reality that many minors will not seek important, sensitive health services if required to inform their parents. Today, a significant body of federal and state law explicitly guarantees confidential access to services or does so by implication. Since its inception in 1970, Title X of the Public Health Service Act—the only federal program dedicated to providing family planning services to low-income women and teenagers—has provided confidential services to people regardless of age (although minors must be encouraged to include their parents in their decision to seek services). The federal Medicaid statute also requires family planning services to be provided confidentially to sexually active minors who seek them.

In stark contrast to the protections generally afforded to minors seeking STD care and contraceptive services, laws addressing minors' access to abortion services are often quite restrictive. Currently, 34 states require that a minor either notify or receive consent from one or both parents prior to obtaining an abortion; 21 states require parental consent, and 13 states require parental notification. However, with the exception of Utah, whose law remains unchallenged, all of the 34 states provide for an alternative process that allows a minor to obtain an abortion without involving a parent, as is constitutionally required. These laws typically either allow a minor to obtain approval from a court (known as a "judicial bypass") or permit another adult relative to be notified of or consent to the procedure. Most laws also include provisions that allow the doctor to forego parental involvement in the case of a medical emergency or in cases of parental abuse, assault, incest or neglect.

Minors' Confidentiality Rights

A regulation issued in 2002 pursuant to requirements of the Health Insurance Portability and Accountability Act (HIPAA) technically vitiates the long-standing presumption that when minors legally consent to medical care, they can also expect their medical records to remain confidential. Under the regulation, minors will only control their medical records when

On Teen Access to Confidential Care

"The potential health risks to adolescents if they are unable to obtain reproductive health services are so compelling that legal barriers and deference to parental involvement should not stand in the way of needed health care for patients who request confidentiality. Therefore, laws and regulations that are unduly restrictive of adolescents' confidential access to reproductive health care should be revised."

The American College of Obstetricians and Gynecologists,
Access to Reproductive Health Care for Adolescents, 2003.

states explicitly authorize them to do so. But when a state is silent on the specific subject of medical records (as most of them now are), the health care provider may decide whether to maintain the confidentiality of those medical records or disclose them to a parent. Thus, a state law granting minors the right to consent to reproductive health care no longer implicitly guarantees the confidentiality of their medical records. Still, it is worth noting that the regulation explicitly states that it "does not want to interfere with the professional requirements . . . or other ethical codes of health care providers with respect to the confidentiality of health information or with the health care practices of such providers with respect to adolescent health care."

Research May Not Support Policies

Proponents of laws and policies designed to require parents to be involved in their adolescent's decisions to seek reproductive health care argue that in addition to restoring "parental rights," such requirements will further parent-child communication while dissuading minors from engaging in sexual activity; however, research spanning almost three decades fails to confirm these claims. There is no research that supports the notion that mandatory parental involvement requirements for either contraceptive services or abortion improve parent-child communication or facilitate conversations about sex, birth control or related matters. To the contrary, the research suggests that these policies are potentially harmful to teenagers' health and well-being, and highlights the importance of confidentiality to teenagers' willingness to seek care.

Surveys of teenagers in family planning clinics have found that approximately half of adolescents report that a parent knows that they were at the clinic, according to a literature review published in 2005 in Current Opinions in Obstetrics and Gynecology. Those who do not want to inform their parents that they are at a clinic, however, give many reasons, including a desire to be self-sufficient and not wanting to disappoint parents.

Research shows that more than six in 10 teenagers in states without a parental consent requirement say one or both parents knew about the abortion, according to a study published in 1992 in Family Planning Perspectives (FPP). A similar study published in 1987 in the American Journal of Public Health (AJPH) found that the proportion of teens who inform their parents is approximately the same in states with and without such requirements. Moreover, there is no evidence to suggest that laws mandating parental involvement in a teenager's decision to obtain an abortion improve family communication or relationships.

In contrast, research suggests that parental consent requirements can have potentially serious adverse consequences associated with delayed access to timely medical care among those teenagers who do not wish to involve their parents in their abortion decisions. Teenagers typically detect their pregnancies later than do adults, and legal obstacles that create further impediments to timely care are likely to result in later abortions, which are significantly more dangerous to a woman's health and more expensive to obtain. Some teenagers seeking an abortion may obtain a judicial bypass; however, obtaining a judicial bypass can take time, inevitably delaying the abortion procedure. Other teenagers may travel to states with less restrictive abortion laws rather than involve a parent, and it can take time for an adolescent to muster the will and resources to undertake an out-of-state trip without a parent's knowledge. A delay also can result when a teenager who is reluctant to inform her parents puts off the dreaded discussion as long as possible. These factors help explain why three separate studies looking at Missouri, Minnesota and Mississippi published between 1991 and 1996 in the AJPH, FPP and Women and Health, respectively, found that minors had later abortions following the enactment of a mandated parental involvement law than was previously the case, with a higher proportion performed in the second trimester (after 12 weeks' gestation).

Parental Involvement Places Teens at Risk

In addition, forcing teenagers to inform their parents that they are pregnant or seeking an abortion may place some at risk of physical violence or abuse. The 1992 FPP study found that approximately one-third of teenagers who did not tell their parents about their decision to seek an abortion had experienced violence in their family, or feared that violence would occur or that they would be forced to leave home. Among minors whose parents found out about their pregnancy from other sources, 6% reported physical violence, being forced to leave home or damage to their parents' health.

Proponents of parental involvement laws claim that such requirements reduce abortion and pregnancy rates among teenagers for two reasons. First, they argue that with their parents' guidance, more pregnant teenagers will choose childbirth (and perhaps adoption) over abortion. Second, they claim that teenagers who do not wish to inform their parents about a pregnancy to obtain an abortion will think twice before having sex in the first place. Studies with findings that appear to support these contentions typically suffer from methodological problems. For example, a 2004 analysis by the Heritage Foundation concluded that parental involvement policies have resulted in modest declines in abortion rates. The analysis, however, ignores the possibility that some young people sought abortions in neighboring states where the laws are less restrictive. In contrast, studies published in AJPH in 1986 and FPP in 1995 demonstrate that while the number of abortions performed on minors falls dramatically in states following the implementation of parental involvement statutes, the number of abortions performed in neighboring states rises accordingly.

Future Litigation

To be sure, the notion of providing confidential reproductive health services to minors remains under attack at the state and federal levels. Legislators in seven states have introduced bills in 2005 requiring parental consent or notification for family planning services. Similarly, the Parents' Right to Know Act, legislation that would require Title X, supported family planning clinics to notify the parents of any minor seeking contraceptives at least five days before dispensing a method, is pending in Congress. With respect to abortion, legislators in 29 states have introduced legislation in 2005 to either impose a new parental involvement requirement or tighten an existing law; bills were signed into law in seven states. In California, a major ballot initiative will go before the voters in November [2005] that would amend the state constitution to require health care providers to notify parents or guardians 48 hours before they perform an abortion on an unmarried minor. (The measure includes an exception for medical emergencies and when a parent or guardian signs a waiver allowing the procedure to happen sooner.) And, at the federal level, the

House of Representatives passed the Child Interstate Abortion Notification Act (CIANA), a complicated and convoluted legislative proposal that would have the effect of imposing a strict federal parental notification requirement that would be applicable even in states that have rejected such a policy. The legislation is now pending before the Senate.

Even more ominous, perhaps, is that the Supreme Court is scheduled to hear the case of *Ayotte v. Planned Parenthood of Northern New England* in November [2005]. The case involves a New Hampshire statute that requires notification of one parent 48 hours before a minor's abortion, or a judicial bypass, with an exception only for situations where a physician can certify that the emergency abortion is necessary to prevent the minor's death. Lower federal courts have held the law unconstitutional because it does not contain an exception for emergency situations where an abortion is necessary to protect the minor's health. The New Hampshire attorney general is arguing that a parental notification law need not have a health exception on the theory that the judicial bypass can function quickly enough to allow for an emergency abortion when a minor's health is at stake. If a newly comprised Court accepts this reasoning, it would upset legal precedents that say that a physician must be able to proceed immediately to protect a minor's health.

It is clear that a great deal is at stake in the coming months that will determine whether many teenagers across the nation are able to obtain confidential contraceptive and abortion services or whether they will be forced to involve their parents. As the research indicates, this has significant implications for teenagers' health and well-being. How all of this plays out, and how teenagers fare as a result, remains to be seen.

> *"The fundamental right of parents to make decisions concerning the care, custody, and control of their children is one of the oldest interests protected by American law."*

Teens Should Not Be Allowed an Abortion Without Parental Consent

Teresa Stanton Collett

In the following viewpoint, Teresa Stanton Collett defends legislators and citizens in their desire to enact legislation that would deny abortion services to girls without first gaining parental consent. In rebuttal to claims by opponents of the legislation, the author makes several assertions, including that parents do not react violently to the teen upon learning of the intent to have an abortion, and that parents' knowledge of an abortion is vital to the girl's health and well-being. Teresa Stanton Collett is a professor of law at the University of St. Thomas School of Law in Minnesota.

Editor's Note: "The Child Custody Prevention Act" (CCPA) and the "Child Interstate Abortion Notification Act" (CIANA) were rejected by the Senate in September 2006.

Teresa Stanton Collett, "Transporting Minors for Immoral Purposes: The Case for the Child Custody Protection Act & the Child Interstate Abortion Notification Act," ssrn.com, January 9, 2006. Reproduced by permission of the author.

As you read, consider the following questions:

1. According to the Henshaw and Kost study as mentioned in the viewpoint, what is the primary reason that minors avoid telling their parents about an unexpected pregnancy?
2. What did the same study find to be the most common reported effect for parents when learning about their child's pregnancy?
3. According to the author, in how many states have legislators passed some form of parental involvement law?

Parents in twenty-eight states are effectively guaranteed the right to be involved in their minor daughters' decisions to obtain abortions in most cases where the abortions are obtained in the minor's state of residence. The Child Custody Protection Act (CCPA) and its companion legislation, the Child Interstate Abortion Notification Act (CIANA), are designed to ensure that these state law protections of minors continue, whether the minor obtains the abortion in her home state or elsewhere. . . .

Study About Parental Involvement Is Flawed

The claim that a majority of teens have involved a parent in their decision to obtain abortions uniformly originates from a study by Stanley Henshaw and Kathryn Kost. The methodology of the study itself is subject to several criticisms. While it purports to be "based on a nationally representative sample of more than 1,500 unmarried minors having an abortion," no respondents from the twenty-one states requiring parental involvement at that time were included. Therefore, no respondent was impacted by a parental consent or notification law. Further, the sample included only respondents who obtained abortions—there is no information from adolescents who decided to continue their pregnancies.

Even more importantly, the study is based only on a survey of adolescents with no attempt to gain information from the parents of the minors. To obtain an accurate understanding of the impact and value of parental involvement in minors' abortion decisions, it is necessary to have information from both the adolescents and their parents. Without information obtained directly from parents of those adolescents who responded to survey questions about their parents, there is no basis for assessing the accuracy of the adolescents' perceptions regarding their parents' knowledge, behavior, and attitudes.

Researcher bias is most evident in the design of the survey. Minors whose parents knew of their pregnancy were asked whether they experienced any of eleven possible "adverse" consequences from their parents finding out, but were not asked about any possible positive outcomes. At a minimum, balanced research would require asking respondents to also report benefits of parents finding out about their intended abortion and whether the minors are glad that their parents were involved in the decision-making process.

Notwithstanding these obvious flaws, the study is extensively relied upon in the debate regarding parental involvement laws. Opponents of such laws commonly cite the study for the proposition that "most teens voluntarily involve their parents in their abortion decision," relying on the fact that 61 percent of minors surveyed claimed a parent knew of their decision to obtain an abortion. Yet according to the study, only 45 percent of the minors had informed a parent of their pregnancy and abortion plans. The remaining parents had learned of the pregnancy and abortion plans from someone other than the minor.

Of the girls under age sixteen whose parents were unaware of their pregnancy, only 47 percent involved "any adult" in their abortion decision or arrangements. For girls ages sixteen and seventeen the percentage involving "any adult" only went up to 52 percent. "By the definitional parameters of Dr.

Henshaw's study, the 'involvement' which the 'any adult' had in the girl's abortion 'arrangements' may have involved only paying for the abortion or driving to the clinic. 'Involvement' did not necessarily include any sort of 'counsel' or emotional support."

Laws Substantially Increase Parental Involvement

With parental involvement laws in effect, the increase in parental involvement is dramatic. In 2004, 771 girls got abortions in Alabama with a parent's approval and fifteen with a judge's approval according to state health department records. Idaho similarly reports only 5 percent using judicial bypass to avoid that state's parental consent law in 2003. South Dakota reports less than 10 percent (six of sixty-six) of the minors obtained judicial bypasses, rather than allow a parent [to] be notified of their intent to obtain an abortion. In Wisconsin, with its more liberal definition of who could provide consent, 85 percent of the minors obtaining abortions had parental consent. In Texas, parental involvement in abortion decision-making by minor girls signifcantly increased, from 69 percent to approximately 95 percent, immediately after enactment of that state's parental notification law. "In Massachusetts, where the state's parental consent law has been in operation for more than twenty years, the number of girls seeking parental bypass has substantially declined from a rate of 900–1000 per year in 1991 to a rate of 450–500 in 2003." With the encouragement of parental involvement laws, a substantial majority of minors include their parents in deciding how to respond to an unexpected pregnancy.

Contrary to the concerns expressed by opponents of CCPA and CIANA, the Henshaw and Kost study found that the primary reason minors avoided telling their parents was not fear of physical violence or abandonment, but a desire to avoid parental disappointment. . . .

Abortion Consent Laws Lower Teens' Risky Sexual Behavior

Florida State University law professor Jonathan Klick said the incidence of at least one sexually transmitted disease (STD)—teen gonorrhea—is dramatically reduced in states that have laws requiring minors to first notify a parent or seek permission before having an abortion....

"We're able to use the passage and repeal of parental involvement laws for abortions to basically look at how teenagers respond to the change in the cost of risky sex." Klick said.

Pete Winn, "Abortion Consent Laws Also Cut Teen STD Rates," Cybercast News Service, October 16, 2007. www.cnsnews.com.

Adolescents are often reluctant to inform their parents about any action that they know would displease or disappoint them. Therefore, it is not surprising that adolescents are fearful of their parents' disapproval or disappointment upon learning of a minor daughter's pregnancy. But such fear does not justify empowering an adolescent to disregard the very people in her life who can provide her with informed, experienced input and sincere, selfless support while responding to an unplanned pregnancy.

Parental Reactions Are Not Violent

The study also identified some effects of parental involvement for those minors who indicated that a parent knew of their intention to obtain an abortion. The most commonly reported effect was that parents' stress increased. Parental stress upon learning of a child's problem is hardly uncommon or indicative of family dysfunction. Another "adverse" result was that parents forced the respondent to stop seeing her boyfriend. It is not clear whether this consequence was harmful to the child; it may have been both beneficial for the child and mutually agreed upon as in her best interests. "[P]arents whose daughters told them about the pregnancy were understanding and supportive as often as they were upset and disappointed." In fact, when parents were told about the pregnancy by their daughter, 87 percent of mothers and 77 percent of fathers were supportive of an abortion, while only 5 percent of the mothers and 6 percent of the fathers were not supportive.

These results comport with the experience in states having parental involvement laws in effect. As part of the preparation for litigation related to the Minnesota parental involvement law, Minnesota Attorney General Hubert Humphrey prepared a memorandum in 1989, which states that "after some five years of the statute's operation, the evidence does not disclose a single instance of abuse or forceful obstruction of abortion for any Minnesota minor." He also noted that the plaintiffs in the case conceded that there was no evidence of any increase in medical complications which could be attributed to the law.

Testimony before the Texas House of Representatives' Committee on State Affairs, when considering the Texas Parental Notification Act, on Massachusetts' experience with its parental consent law revealed a similar absence of unintended, but harmful, consequences. Ms. Jamie Sabino, chair of the Massachusetts Judicial Consent for Minors Lawyer Referral Panel, could identify no case of a Massachusetts minor being abused or abandoned as a result of that state's law. In response to questioning, she also testified that there had been no increase in the number of illegal abortions in Massachusetts since the enactment of the statute in 1981. . . .

Fears of Injury from Illegal Abortions Are Unsupported

Some opponents may be willing to accept that parental involvement laws provide a necessary incentive for a significant number of teens whose primary objection to having their parents know they are pregnant is embarrassment and fear of parental disappointment, yet these opponents still object on the basis of what they agree would be a rare case of a minor who might injure herself by attempting to self-induce an abortion or seek an illegal abortion.

Similar arguments have been asserted before in debates regarding other abortion regulations. They ultimately have proven groundless. When the Hyde Amendment, which restricted governmental funding for abortions, was first being considered Dr. Willard Cates, representing the Centers for Disease Control Abortion Surveillance Branch, predicted a total of seventy-seven excess deaths to women who would seek illegal abortions and an additional five excess deaths due to delays in seeking abortion. The same department would later admit that no such increase in mortality or morbidity had occurred. Even Dr. Cates later admitted that "nationally, there were only two deaths following illegal abortions in 1976, four in 1977, seven in 1978, none in 1979 and 'we think one [or] two in 1980 and one so far in 1981.' One death, he said, is 'directly attributable' and three are 'indirectly attributable' to lack of federal funds."

This experience, combined with the experience of states having parental involvement laws with no ill effects on the well-being of minors—some for over two decades—suggests that injuries from self-induced or illegal abortions is largely a phantom fear.

Parental Involvement Is Vital for Girls' Health

Testimony regarding families' experiences absent parental involvement laws, as well as the medical literature concerning women's health, suggest that there are many medical benefits from requiring parental involvement.

First and foremost, parental involvement laws ensure that parents have adequate knowledge to assist their daughters in responding to any post-abortion complications that may arise. When considering the Texas Parental Notification Act, legislators heard several stories of parents whose ability to respond to their daughters' medical crises were limited by not knowing of their daughters' abortions. Leslie French, a nineteen year-old student at the University of Texas testified regarding "Amy," who was fifteen and pregnant. Amy obtained an abortion on Friday, suffered terrible complications, and subsequently died on Sunday. Because Amy's parents did not know of her abortion, they delayed taking her to hospital until she was unconscious. Hospital personnel originally told the parents that Amy died of septic shock syndrome, but one of her friends who knew of the abortion told them after Amy's death. The parents then confirmed her death was due to complications from the abortion. Healthcare providers explained that they initially refused to discuss the abortion as the cause of death because of their concern for Amy's right to privacy. . . .

In New Jersey, legislators considering a state constitutional amendment to ensure parental involvement heard the story of another young girl who died because her parents did not know of her abortion. Alda Atkinson told the story of

> a [fifteen]-year-old who came home from school not feeling well, [laid] down on the couch, and during the night she quietly bled to death. [The parents] had no idea what was the cause. And eventually, some of [the girl's] friends came forward to say she had an abortion. It was actually her second.

Both Congress and the federal courts have received similar testimony of the harm suffered from the inability of parents to effectively respond to minors' secret abortions. Parental notice or consent laws, including CCPA and CIANA, are aimed at preventing such tragedies. . . .

A Secret Abortion Is Not a Constitutional Right

The final argument that opponents of the CCPA and CIANA raise are related to the proper limits on federal power:

> Allowing a state's laws to extend beyond its borders runs completely contrary to the state sovereignty principles on which this country is founded. For example, gambling using slot machines is legal in the state of Nevada, but not in California [outside American Indian gaming facilities]. Residents of Nevada are prohibited from gambling while in California, while California residents of those states are permitted to gamble while in Nevada. Forcing citizens of California to carry their home state's law into Nevada, thereby prohibiting them from using slot machines while in Nevada, would be inconsistent with federalism principles. Requiring compliance within the borders of one state with the different and possibly conflicting law of another state would be even more ludicrous in the case of abortion—a constitutionally protected right—than it would be in the case of casino gambling, which is not a constitutionally protected activity.

Inherent in this argument are a number of assumptions, chief among them that a minor's obtaining a secret abortion is a "constitutionally protected activity" and that this activity trumps the historically recognized constitutional right of parents to direct the care and upbringing of their minor children. Both assumptions have little basis in the Supreme Court's current interpretation of the Constitution.

In *H.L. v. Matheson* [1981], the Court specifically rejected the idea that "every minor, regardless of age or maturity, may give effective consent for termination of her pregnancy." As Justice [John Paul] Stevens has observed, the Supreme Court "has never challenged a State's reasonable judgment that [a minor's abortion] decision should be made after notification to and consultation with a parent." There simply is no right for all minors to obtain secret abortions found in the Constitution or its judicial interpretation.

In contrast, "the fundamental right of parents to make decisions concerning the care, custody, and control of their children" is one of the oldest interests protected by American law. The Court's repeated affirmations of this right have firmly established it as having constitutional magnitude. . . .

State Laws Extend Beyond Borders

Given that states clearly have the constitutional authority to enact parental involvement laws, the only question posed by the CCPA and CIANA is whether Congress can pass legislation giving them extraterritorial effect. Professor Mark Rosen addressed this issue in his testimony before a Congressional Subcommittee:

> First, [the CCPA] can be conceptualized as a federal law extension to state law that functions to increase the state law's efficacy. So understood, [the CCPA] does not extend the operation of state law extraterritorially, but simply is federal law that operates across state borders, as federal law often does.
>
> Second, the criticism that [the CCPA] unlawfully extends state laws is based on the misconception that one state's regulatory authority ends at its borders. An early approach to choice-of-law believed that territorial location alone answered the question of what law applies, but this has been almost universally rejected in this country. Today, state laws regularly apply to persons, transactions, and occurrences that occur outside the state's borders. Thus scholarly restatements of the law and the Model Penal Code [text of standardized U.S. penal law] both understand that states may regulate their citizens' out-of-state activities, and may even criminalize out-of-state activity that is permissible in the state where it occurs. . . .

Experience has shown that parental involvement laws decrease teen pregnancy and increase the ability of responsible parents to guide and support their minor daughters during this difficult time. They protect the health of minors by ensuring that parents had adequate information to monitor and respond knowledgably to any post-abortion complications that arise. Such laws also assure the ability of parents to intervene in cases where their young daughters are being victimized by adult males who seek to conceal the consequences of their sexual conduct by persuading the girls to obtain secret abortions. Legislators in forty-five states have recognized the value of parental involvement in a minor's decision to obtain an abortion and have passed some form of parental involvement law. The CCPA and CIANA simply furthers the ability of states to protect their minor citizens and the rights of parents to be involved in the decisions of their daughters who are facing unplanned pregnancies.

Periodical Bibliography

The following articles have been selected to supplement the diverse views presented in this chapter.

Kelly Boggs — "Please, Portland, Let Them Be Kids," *Baptist Press*, October 19, 2007.

Jane Clifford — "Giving Your Kid a Map for the Sexual Minefield," *San Diego Union Tribune*, December 22, 2007.

Crimson Staff — "Contraception in Middle School? Portland's School Board Has Overstepped Its Boundaries," *Harvard Crimson*, October 21, 2007.

Kristen Fyfe — "Middle School Kids Are Having Sex! Rather Than a Call for Contraception, Shouldn't That Be a Wakeup Call to Our Culture?" Culture and Media Institute, October 18, 2007.

Nancy Gibbs — "Birth Control for Kids?" *Time*, October 18, 2007.

Ellen Goodman — "Teen Pregnancies and Cultural Wars," *Boston Globe*, January 4, 2008.

Valerie Huber — "Opposing View: Abstinence Works," *USA Today*, July 30, 2007.

Ruth Marcus — "Learning from Jamie Lynn and Juno," *Washington Post*, December 28, 2007.

Jennifer Roback Morse — "Get the Government Out of Sex Ed," Townhall.com, July 9, 2007.

MaryLee Shrider — "Birth Control for Kids Ought to Cause Fuss," *Bakersfield Californian*, November 16, 2007.

Pete Winn — "Abortion Consent Laws Also Cut Teen STD Rates," CNSNews.com, October 16, 2007.

How Can Society Deal with Teenage Crime and Violence?

Chapter Preface

"Old enough to do the crime; old enough to do the time." The phrase was made popular by politicians and prosecutors in the 1980s and 1990s during an explosion of juvenile violent crime—the teen murder arrest rate increased 110 percent between 1987 and 1993. In response, state legislatures lowered the age and expanded the list of crimes for which juvenile offenders could be tried as adults in criminal court instead of in the more rehabilitative-oriented juvenile justice system. However, recent research on the adolescent brain, which indicates that juveniles are not fully mature in their judgment, problem-solving, and decision-making capabilities, as well as studies that reveal an increase in recidivism rates among teens sentenced as adults, have caused juvenile justice experts and many state lawmakers to reconsider how juvenile offenders should be treated. In fact, a 2007 national poll commissioned by the MacArthur Foundation and the Center for Children's Law and Policy found widespread public support for the juvenile justice system to focus on rehabilitating teens rather than imprisoning them. As juvenile center research expert Melissa Sickmund said, "If you do good in juvenile justice, you won't have adult criminals."

In New York, Judge Michael Corriero agrees. He believes an ideal system would unite both the juvenile and criminal courts toward a common goal: the rehabilitation of youth to become responsible, productive, law-abiding citizens. Judge Corriero wrote in his book *Judging Children as Children*, "The method of prosecution and punishment adopted by a community must be flexible enough to recognize and accommodate juveniles who have the capacity to change their behavior." State Attorney Harry Shorstein of Jacksonville, Florida, says he has created his own juvenile justice system. "The secret is not choosing punishment versus prevention, but using both." And the Council of the City of New York wrote in a report about juvenile crime, "Sentencing of violent adolescent offenders can and must be multifaceted—at once punitive, incapacitative, and rehabilitative. Every component of the juvenile justice system must reflect these integrated goals."

Psychologists and brain researchers have learned that violent tendencies can be outgrown; most violent teenagers do not necessarily turn into violent adults. Thus, an important objective for juvenile justice reform should be flexibility in sentencing laws to determine which juveniles are malleable enough to learn from their mistakes and change their behavior through alternative preventive programs. According to Judge Corriero, the juvenile court should be used as a screening device, sending only the most incorrigible juvenile offenders to the adult criminal court. Considering that approximately six hundred thousand people—most with no job skills or strong family ties—are released from prison every year, society can only benefit from juvenile justice reform that would incorporate education, job training, and therapeutic treatment while incarcerated. In the words of President George W. Bush, "America is the land of [the] second chance, and when the gates of prison open, the path ahead should lead to a better life."

Reforming the juvenile justice system is one of many issues concerning crime and adolescents. The authors in the following chapter discuss other ways to reduce teen crime and violence, such as zero tolerance laws and gun control legislation.

> *"Death of and injury to America's children and youth are undeniably linked to the presence and availability of handguns, particularly in America's homes."*

Gun Control Legislation Reduces Teenage Crime and Violence

Bert H. Deixler

Bert H. Deixler contends in the following viewpoint that more children and young adults in America die due to handguns than by almost any other cause of death, and that access to guns in the home increases the risk of both accidental injuries as well as intentional shootings. He, therefore, insists that the handgun ban in the District of Columbia must be upheld to prevent an increase in the number of children harmed by firearms. Bert H. Deixler submitted a Brief of Amici Curiae to the U.S. Court of Appeals for the District of Columbia in support of maintaining the handgun ban that was enacted there in 1976.

Bert H. Deixler, "On Writ of Certiorari to the United States Court of Appeals for the District of Columbia Circuit, Brief of the American Academy of Pediatrics, The Society for Adolescent Medicine, the Children's Defense Fund, Women Against Gun Violence, and Youth Alive! as Amici Curiae in support of petitioners in the case of the District of Columbia and Adrian M. Fenty, Mayor of the District of Columbia, Petitioners, v. Dick Anthony Heller, Respondent," January 11, 2008.

Editor's Note: In a 5–4 decision on June 26, 2008, the U.S. Supreme Court overturned Washington, D.C.'s ban on handgun possession.

As you read, consider the following questions:

1. Why do handguns pose a unique danger to children and adolescents, according to the author?

2. As stated by the author, where do 89 percent of childhood unintentional shooting deaths occur?

3. According to Deixler, how does the firearms death rate in the United States compare to that of other democratic nations?

The District of Columbia reasonably has enacted legislation to attempt to curtail death among its children and adolescents by preventing lawful access to a principal means of the cause of death: handguns. The prohibition of access to a young person's death delivery system reflects the multiple realities of the fascination handguns hold for children, the proven failure of gun safety education, and the lethal character of those weapons.

Consistent with the responsibilities of municipal government confronted with a public health crisis among its most vulnerable, the District of Columbia enacted [in 1976] narrow legislation [banning private possession of handguns] to staunch the contagion. Moreover, available statistics demonstrate the success of the District of Columbia's legislative formula among the youthful group most affected. No less restrictive alternative could reasonably be expected to be as successful in controlling the health crisis among the afflicted youthful group. Nothing in the jurisprudence of this Court, or in the intentions of the Framers [of the U.S. Constitution], can mandate a reading of the Second Amendment to require a municipality to abandon a successful, reasonable public health measure and substitute a policy certain to increase the risk that the most vulnerable will be the most harmed.

Handguns Are More Lethal than Other Firearms

Handguns are strikingly more lethal than other types of firearms. Of the one million Americans who died by firearms violence between 1962 and 1994, more than two out of three were killed by handguns—a total of more than 670,000 unnecessary deaths. Yet, although handguns are responsible for approximately two-thirds of all deaths by firearms violence, handguns only account for one-third of the 192 million firearms owned in America. Thus, the majority of American gun owners own either a rifle or a shotgun. As these statistics demonstrate, while fewer in number, handguns are more lethal than other types of firearms and disproportionately responsible for firearms deaths in America.

Handguns are more likely than any other type of gun to be used in interpersonal violence and crime, as well as self-directed injury. Indeed, handguns are used in nearly 70 percent of firearms suicides and 75 percent of firearms homicides in the United States. Further, handguns account for 77 percent of all traced guns used in crime.

While these statistics reflect the devastating impact of handguns on people of all ages, handguns pose a unique danger to children and adolescents. Handguns are light, portable, and easy to handle—they are also accessible, romanticized in media, accessible to adolescents, and fascinating to children. Seventy-five percent of 8–12-year-old boys will handle a gun when they find one, and approximately half of those will pull the trigger—even if they have been told about gun safety. There is simply no way to make guns "safe" for children—gun safety programs have little effect in reducing firearms death and injury. Death of and injury to America's children and youth are undeniably linked to the presence and availability of handguns, particularly in America's homes.

Facts About Children Killed by Firearms

Since 1979 gun violence has snuffed out the lives of **101,413 children and teens** in America:

- These 101,413 children and teens would fill 4,056 public school classrooms of 25 students each.

- 101,413 child and teen gun deaths is more than the total number of American fatalities in all wars since World War II ended including the Korean, Vietnam, Iraq and Afghanistan conflicts.

- The number of Black children and teens killed by gunfire is more than 10 times the number of Black citizens of all ages lynched throughout American history.

Children's Defense Fund,
"Protect Children, Not Guns," 2007. www.childrensdefense.org.

Handguns in the Home Are Deadly to Children

A study conducted in 2005 revealed that over 1.69 million children under age 18 are living in homes with *loaded* and *unlocked* firearms. In fact, an estimated one out of three handguns is kept loaded and unlocked. In one 2006 study, 73 percent of children under age 10 reported knowing the location of their parents' firearms and 36 percent admitted that they had handled the weapons. Accordingly, it is not surprising that 89 percent of childhood unintentional shooting deaths occur in the home, or that most of these deaths occur when children are playing with a loaded gun in their parents' absence.

Moreover, contrary to the popular myth that guns are necessary in the home for self-defense, one study found that there are four unintentional shootings, seven criminal assaults or homicides, and 11 attempted or completed suicides for every time a gun kept in the home is used in self-defense.

It is simply undeniable that access to firearms in the home increases the risk of both accidental injuries as well as intentional shootings. A study of youth suicide found that more than 75 percent of guns used by youth in suicide attempts and unintentional injuries were kept in the home of the victim, a relative, or a friend. Another study, published by the U.S. Secret Service, of 37 school shootings in 26 states found that, in more than 65 percent of the cases, the shooter got the gun from his or her home or that of a relative.

Handguns are also undeniably the "firearm of choice" among teens. A 1996 survey of high school students by the National Institute of Justice found that high-school aged youth who carried guns outside the home most frequently carried an automatic or semiautomatic handgun (50 percent) and next most likely carried a revolver (30 percent). In addition, of those students who admitted to carrying a gun, 43 percent indicated that they were carrying a gun as protection, while 36 percent boasted [of] . . . carrying a gun to "scare someone" or "get back at someone." Most significantly, 52 percent of the armed youth stated that they had received or borrowed a gun from a family member or had taken it from their home without their parent's permission.

Because of the inherent developmental and behavioral vulnerabilities of adolescents—such as belief in invincibility, curiosity, and impulsiveness—researchers have determined that gun safety education is not likely to prevent firearms death and injury in teenagers and younger children. The simple and frightening truth is, when children find guns, they play with them.

In 1988, the National Rifle Association launched the Eddie Eagle GunSafe Program to teach children in pre-K [prekindergarten] through third grade four important steps to take if they find a gun. The program's mascot, Eddie Eagle, informs children what to do if they see a gun: (1) STOP!; (2) Don't Touch; (3) Leave the Area; and (4) Tell an Adult. Evaluations of the Eddie Eagle GunSafe Program found that while the campaign may teach 4–7 year olds to repeat safety messages, the messages do not lead to actual changes in the children's behaviour. . . .

Children Are Often Victims of Unintentional Shootings

The increased accessibility to handguns that will result if the District of Columbia handgun ban is struck down will increase the number of children who will be harmed in accidents involving firearms. Studies have shown that fewer than half of United States families with both firearms and children maintain the firearms separate from ammunition. This practice is especially troubling because children as young as three are able to pull the trigger of most handguns. Approximately 70 percent of all unintentional firearms injuries and deaths are a result of handguns.

Unintentional firearms death disproportionately affects children: In 2004, firearms accounted for 27 percent of the unintentional deaths among youth aged 10–19, while accounting for only 22 percent of unintentional deaths among the population as a whole. Additionally, between 2000 and 2004, 143 to 193 children were killed each year from unintentional shootings. Most unintentional firearms-related deaths among children occur in or around the home—50 percent at the home of the victim and 40 percent at the home of a friend or relative—and occur when children play with loaded and accessible guns. Moreover, between 2000 and 2004, 22,864 children sustained unintentional, non-fatal firearms-related injuries.

The more guns a jurisdiction has, the more likely children in that jurisdiction will die from a firearm accident. In a study of accidental firearms deaths that occurred between 1979 and 1999, children aged four and under were 17 times more likely to die from a gun accident in the four states with the most guns versus the four states with the fewest guns. Thus, if the handgun ban in the District of Columbia is struck down, the number of children who will die or be injured by handguns accidentally will increase significantly. . . .

Availability of Handguns Increases Homicide Rate

Nationally, children and young adults are killed by firearms more frequently than almost any other cause of death. In 2004, firearms homicide was the second leading cause of injury death for persons 15 to 24 years of age, second only to motor vehicle crashes. Incredibly, in that same year, firearms homicide—not car accidents—was the leading cause of death for African American males between the ages of 15 and 34.

Children and youth are murdered with handguns more often than by all other weapons combined. And, for every child murdered by a gun, four more sustain firearm assault injury.

Firearms (particularly handguns) also represent the leading weapon utilized by both children and adults in the commission of homicide. Between 1985 and 2002, the firearms homicide death rate increased 36 percent for homicides committed by 15 to 19 year olds nationwide. In each year after 1985, handguns have been the most used homicide weapon by juveniles (those age 17 and under) nationwide. Scholars note that the dramatic increase in the rate of homicide committed by juveniles is attributable largely to the increase in attacks with firearms. University of California, Berkeley law professor

Franklin Zimring has observed, "the most important reason for the sharp escalation in homicide [among offenders thirteen to seventeen] was an escalating volume of fatal attacks with firearms."

Importantly, researchers at the Institute of Criminal Justice and Criminology at the University of Maryland found that gun-related homicides in the District of Columbia dropped 25 percent after the enactment of the ban. Statistics also reveal that on America's elementary and secondary school campuses, where guns are banned, a relatively low incidence of gun-related violence is reported. For example, in each year between 1992 and 2000, children and youth aged five to 19 were at least 70 times more likely to be murdered away from school than at school. College campuses also reflect similarly lower rates for on-campus as compared to off-campus violence.

U.S. Firearm Death Rates Are Higher than in Other Countries

The firearms death rate in the United States far surpasses that of other democratic nations. A 1997 study analyzing firearms deaths for children aged 14 or under in 26 industrialized countries found that 86 percent of all deaths occurred in the United States. The rate for firearms homicide alone was 16 times higher in the United States, while the firearms suicide rate was 11 times higher and the firearms unintentional death rate was nine times higher.

In 1995, the firearms death rate in the United States was 13.7 per 100,000. In comparison, the firearms death rates in countries that severely limit access to handguns were significantly lower. For example, in 1995, Canada had a firearms death rate of 3.9 per 100,000; Australia had a rate of 2.9 per 100,000; and England and Wales had rates of 0.4 per 100,000. One of the most glaring distinctions between these countries and the United States is the significantly lower incidents of lethal violence caused by handguns. For instance, handgun homicide rates are 15.3 times higher in the United States than in Canada. For 1989–95, the average handgun homicide rate was 4.8 per 100,000 in the U.S., compared to 0.3 per 100,000 in Canada.

In addition, while adolescents in other industrialized countries are just as likely as adolescents in the United States to engage in violent behavior, such as fighting and weapon carrying, violence related mortality in the United States is substantially higher than that of other industrialized countries. This can be explained, in large part, by the ease with which adolescents in the United States have access to firearms compared to adolescents in other such countries. . . .

Because of the proven harm attributable to handguns and especially because of the unique risk handguns create for children and adolescents, the District of Columbia reasonably enacted legislation [ban on handguns] to mitigate a pervasive public health crisis. The reasonableness of the District of Columbia's attempt to preserve the public's health is confirmed by both domestic and foreign data. Neither the precedents of this Court, nor the intention of the Framers of the Constitution support striking down the District of Columbia's ordinance.

Editor's Note: On June 26, 2008, the Supreme Court ruled that Americans have a right to own guns for self-defense and hunting, the justices' first major pronouncement on gun rights in U.S. history. The court's 5-4 ruling struck down the District of Columbia's 32-year-old ban on handguns as incompatible with gun rights under the Second Amendment.

> "Since 1976, the District of Columbia has had the most restrictive gun control laws anywhere in the country, and yet during that time it has become notorious as perhaps the nation's worst locus of gun violence."

Gun Control Legislation Does Not Reduce Crime

Peter J. Ferrara

In the following viewpoint, Peter J. Ferrara insists that the Second Amendment to the U.S. Constitution forbids the District of Columbia from banning the private possession of handguns. He further argues that the handgun ban—enacted in the District of Columbia in 1976 to reduce crime—has actually increased the crime rate, and that gun control laws limit the ability of law-abiding citizens to defend themselves. Peter J. Ferrara, the counsel of record for the American Civil Rights Union, submitted a Brief of Amicus Curiae to the U.S. Court of Appeals for the District of Columbia in support of overturning the handgun ban.

Peter J. Ferrara, Counsel of Record, "Interest of the Amicus Curiae," by the American Civil Rights Union in case No. 07-290, District of Columbia and Adrian M. Fenty, Mayor of the District of Columbia, Petitioners, v. Dick Anthony Heller, Respondent, ACRU.org, September 2007.

As you read, consider the following questions:

1. After the handgun ban was enacted in the District of Columbia, what was the change in the murder rate compared with other cities with more than five hundred thousand people, as stated in the viewpoint?

2. Name two reasons cited in the viewpoint that explain how ownership of guns by law-abiding citizens actually results in less crime, according to John Lott in his book *More Guns, Less Crime.*

3. What two states along with the District of Columbia does the author claim completely ban citizens from carrying concealed handguns?

The text of the Second Amendment plainly protects a right of each individual citizen to keep and bear arms, and there is no other logical interpretation of the Amendment.

The text of the Amendment states in part, "The right of the people to keep and bear arms shall not be infringed." This phrase clearly protects a right of each individual citizen to keep and bear arms. As a matter of plain English, there is nothing in the introductory phrase of the Amendment, "A well-regulated militia being necessary to the security of a free people," that puts any limitation on the right granted by the rest of the Amendment. . . .

The courts cannot treat the Second Amendment as a politically incorrect, disfavored stepchild of the Bill of Rights. Fidelity to the Constitution requires that the Judicial branch give it the same zealous protection as every other right stated in our founding document. The Amendment is not being read broadly to protect the rights and liberties of the people if it is somehow interpreted to allow the government to adopt a virtually complete ban on the right to keep and bear arms, or on any particular armament protected under the Amendment, as in this case.

Petitioners [District of Columbia and its mayor, Adrian M. Fenty] argue that regardless of what the Constitution says, the District of Columbia's prohibition on handguns, and its other gun control laws, have been effective in reducing crime and other harms. Therefore, they insist, these gun prohibitions cannot reasonably be found to infringe on the Constitutional right to keep and bear arms.

Gun Control Laws Do Not Reduce Crime

Regardless of the District's policy arguments, the Constitution and the Second Amendment govern. Nevertheless, the District's policy arguments are plain wrong. The District's ban on handguns has not been effective in reducing crime. The fundamental problem is that the District does not have the practical power to take guns away from criminals. At the same time, the District's ban on handguns and other gun control laws have taken guns for self defense out of the hands of law abiding citizens. As a result, the District's gun control restrictions have more likely increased crime.

In the five years before the District banned handguns in 1976, the murder rate fell from 37 to 27 per 100,000. In the five years after the ban, the murder rate rose back up to 35. Indeed, the murder rate in D.C. has been higher than in 1976 in every year since then except one, 1985. From 1977 to 2003, the District's violent crime rate was higher than before 1976 in every year but two. Moreover, after adopting the 1976 handgun ban, the rate of murder and violent crime rose in the District relative to nearby Maryland and Virginia, and to other cities with more than 500,000 people. Indeed, after the handgun ban, D.C. regularly ranked first in murder rates for cities over 500,000.

The same experience with handgun bans has been suffered elsewhere. Chicago's murder rate was dropping before it

Nationwide Comparison of Gun Ownership to Murder Rate

Year	Guns per 1000 persons	Murders per 1000 persons
1946	344	0.069
1950	381	0.053
1960	431	0.051
1970	549	0.079
1980	738	0.101
1990	853	0.094
2000	885	0.055
2001	876	0.056
2002	867	0.056
2003	858	0.057
2004	850	0.055

These figures discredit the theory that predicts increased murder from an increase in guns.

TAKEN FROM: FBI Uniform Crime Reports; Bureau of Alcohol, Tobacco, Firearms and Explosives (BATF) Annual Firearms Manufactures and Export Report.

banned handguns in 1982. The city's murder rate subsequently rose from 5.5 times as large as in the 5 neighboring counties to 12 times as large.

Great Britain banned handguns in 1997. But deaths and injuries from gun crimes in England and Wales rose 340% from 1998 to 2005. Armed robberies, rapes, homicides, and other serious violent crimes also soared.

Ireland banned all handguns and center fire rifles in 1972, but by 1974 murder rates had increased by 5 times. In the 20 years after 1972, the murder rate in Ireland averaged 114% higher than before. Similarly, after Jamaica banned all guns in 1974, murder rates almost doubled from 11.5 per 100,000 in 1973 to 19.5 in 1977, doubling again to 41.7 in 1980.

Public Ownership of Guns Reduces Crime

The reason for this was explained in the seminal, peer-reviewed work, John R. Lott, Jr., *More Guns, Less Crime*. That book showed through extensive econometric analysis that more widespread ownership of guns among the law abiding public actually results in less crime, because criminals are deterred by the fear of encountering a gun owner, and because gun owners often stop crimes in progress.

Lott's position is extensively supported by other research showing that where the law has allowed for increased ownership and possession of functional firearms crime has been reduced. . . .

Crimes involving multiple victim public shootings show the largest drop with conceal and carry policies because, as compared to other violent crimes where only one or at most a few potential victims are present, there is a relatively large chance that one of the potential victims will have a weapon that can be used to defend all of them.

If crime rates in neighboring counties on opposite sides of state borders are compared, the counties in conceal and carry states experience a drop in violent crime at the same time that their neighboring counties across state borders suffer an increase. Indeed, the drop in violent crime in the counties in conceal and carry states is generally four times as large as the increase in violent crime in the counties in other states.

Most States Allow Handgun Permits

Because of overwhelming, compelling evidence like this, 40 states now have conceal and carry permits. Only Wisconsin and Illinois, along with D.C., completely ban citizens from carrying concealed handguns.

Moreover, while Petitioners assert that the nation's three largest cities follow the same gun control policies as the District, that is not true. Los Angeles does not ban handguns, New York City allows conceal and carry permits, and no city prohibits the effective use of rifles and shotguns in self-defense as the District does. Indeed, since 1976, the District of Columbia has had the most restrictive gun control laws anywhere in the country, and yet during that time it has become notorious as perhaps the nation's worst locus of gun violence. . . .

There Is No Justification to Restrict the Second Amendment

Since the District cannot show that its ban on handguns has reduced crime, and, indeed, it probably has increased crime based on the academic literature, the District cannot argue that the ban is a reasonable restriction on the right to keep and bear arms. Indeed, the District has not shown anywhere, and cannot show, that its handgun ban has reduced access to such guns by criminals. As a result, all of the statistics the District cites regarding use of handguns by criminals to commit crimes are irrelevant. They cannot justify the handgun ban if the ban does not reduce access to guns by criminals. And if the ban does not reduce access to guns by criminals, it cannot be a reasonable restriction on the right to keep and bear arms.

Petitioners also repeatedly argue that the handgun ban is reasonable because it only bans one type of weapon, and citizens are still free to utilize rifles and shotguns for self-defense and other uses. But this assertion contradicts the record and the decision below. Again, D.C. Code Section 7-2507.02 requires "that all lawfully owned firearms be kept unloaded and disassembled or bound by a trigger lock or similar device." This section, by its very terms, prevents the use of rifles and shotguns as well as for self-defense and other uses. Moreover, in any event, it denies citizens access to functional firearms for self-defense and possibly other uses. Even less extreme gun lock regulations in other states have been associated with more violent crime because locking the guns makes self defense difficult.

Indeed, again the Court below ruled that this very provision as applied to handguns is unconstitutional because it prevents those weapons from being used for self-defense and other uses. This provision applied to rifles and shotguns would have this same effect as well. Therefore, it cannot be said that under the District's gun control laws citizens are free to use rifles and shotguns for self-defense and other uses.

Accidental Deaths of Children from Handguns Are Rare

Petitioners also argue that the handgun ban is reasonable because the availability of handguns results in accidents causing death, frequently involving children. But lethal handgun accidents are actually quite rare. With 100 million gun owners across the nation in 2004, there were only 649 reported cases of accidental gun deaths.

Moreover, among the 40 million children in the U.S. under the age of 10, the Centers for Disease Control [and Prevention] report 20 accidental gun deaths in 2003. Another 36 accidental gun deaths were reported for children between 10 and 14. Children are 41 times more likely to die from accidental suffocation, 32 times more likely to die from accidental drowning, and 20 times more likely to die due to accidental fires. Of course, random accidents can never be used to justify abridgement of a constitutional right, all the more so when the incidence is so rare.

Editor's Note: On June 26, 2008, the U.S. Supreme Court voted 5–4 in favor of striking down Washington, D.C.'s ban on handgun possession, stating it violates the Second Amendment.

> "Variations of the 'zero tolerance' mentality within the schools and elsewhere have not only taken us back more than 100 years as far as juvenile justice policy is concerned, but [they have] . . . , more importantly, 'widened the net' of social control in that more and more minor offenses are now being processed formally by the police and the juvenile court."

Zero Tolerance Laws Are Unfair

Randall G. Shelden

In the following viewpoint, Randall G. Shelden describes how the school disciplinary approach of zero tolerance has become so out of control that minor school offenses, such as talking out of turn and violating the dress code, have resulted in student arrests. Shelden contends that American society is abandoning youth— especially minority youth—to the prison system instead of investing in them through community involvement. Randall G. Shelden is a professor in the criminal justice department at the

Randall G. Shelden, "Zero Tolerance Run Amok," SheldenSays.com, February 29, 2004. Reproduced by permission.

University of Nevada, Las Vegas, and has published several articles and books about juvenile justice, including Delinquency and Juvenile Justice in American Society.

As you read, consider the following questions:

1. According to one report cited by Shelden, can student lockers be searched without warning in most U.S. high schools?
2. In the 1990s, did the number of serious crimes that were referred to juvenile court, such as robbery and rape, increase or decrease, according to court statistics mentioned in the viewpoint?
3. As cited by the author, how many of the violators of the "safe school ordinance" in Toledo, Ohio, have been minority youth?

In recent years "law and order" politicians have stoked the fears of the public with their rhetoric about the new "menace" of teen "super-predators." Despite the fact that serious crime among juveniles has dropped in recent years, many politicians continue the "get tough" talk. "Zero tolerance" is one of the new mantras. Variations of the "zero tolerance" mentality within the schools and elsewhere have not only taken us back more than 100 years as far as juvenile justice policy is concerned, but [they have] . . . , more importantly, "widened the net" of social control in that more and more minor offenses are now being processed formally by the police and the juvenile court.

Zero Tolerance Run Amok

Some examples: (1) a five-year prison sentence handed out to a 17-year-old Texas high school basketball player who "threw an elbow" to the head of an opposing player in a basketball [game]; (2) two six-year-old children were suspended for three days for playing "cops and robbers" with their fingers (pretending their fingers were guns and going "bang, bang" toward other children); (3) a girl who gave a friend a Nuprin [ibuprofen pill] was suspended for "dealing drugs"; (4) some high school baseball players were suspended for possessing "dangerous weapons" on school grounds—a teacher who suspected them of having drugs found none, but instead found some baseball bats in their cars; (5) a 14-year-old boy was charged by school police with a felony for "throwing a deadly missile" which turned out to be a Halloween "trick or treat" of throwing an egg. He was taken away in handcuffs and put in juvenile detention; (6) in Florida, a 6-year-old was charged with trespassing when he took a shortcut through the schoolyard on his way home (how many of us did that as a kid?); (7) in Indianola, Mississippi, elementary school children have been arrested for talking during assemblies; (8) in Spokane, Washington, three boys were suspended for bringing 2-inch-long "action figure toy guns" to school; (9) a 13-year-old girl in Massachusetts was expelled for having an empty lipstick tube in her purse—this was considered a "potential weapon"; (10) in Texas a "model student" was expelled when officials found a blunt-tipped bread knife in the back of his pickup, left there by his grandmother.

Among the most recent incidents comes from Toledo, Ohio, where school officials have engaged in perhaps the most absurd forms of zero tolerance. According to a *New York Times* story (Jan. 4 [2004]), on October 17 [2003] a 14-year-old girl was handcuffed by the police and hauled off to the local juvenile court. Her "crime" was the clothes she was wearing: "a low-cut midriff top under an unbuttoned sweater," which was a "clear violation of the dress code." The school offered to have her wear a bowling shirt, but she refused. Her mother came in and gave her an oversize T-shirt, which the girl also refused to wear, saying that it "was real ugly." According to the story, the girl is one of the more than two dozen arrested in school this past October [2003] for such "crimes" as "loud and disruptive," "cursing at school officials," and "shouting at class-mates" and, of course, violating the dress code. Such "crimes" are violations of the city's "safe school ordinance."

"Making Schools Like Prisons"

In schools all over the country there has been a swelling of arrests by school police, mostly on minor charges, typically appearing within the "miscellaneous" category, after serious assaults, property crimes and drugs have been totaled in annual reports. One study found that between 1999 and 2001 there was a 300% increase in student arrests in the Miami-Dade [Florida] public school system. Where I live, the school district police have reported increasing arrests for "crimes" placed in this miscellaneous category, going from about 80% of the total to more than 90% in the past ten years. Such draconian measures have been put in place despite the fact that schools are the safest places for children and serious crime on school grounds had been declining long before such policies went into effect.

Schools have often been described as "day prisons" as they often have had that drab look of a prison and plenty of fences all around. These days it has become even worse, as a growing number of reports have noted. One recent report noted that many high school students are complaining that we are "making schools like prisons." This perceptive account further notes that: "Most U.S. high school students will have to walk by numerous hidden cameras, outdoors and indoors, and go through an institutional-size metal detector manned by guards just to get into school each morning. Once there, students are subject to random searches of their bodies and belongings. Lockers can be searched without warning with or without the student present, and in many places police will use drug-sniffing dogs during raids where they search lockers and even students' parked cars."

A law suit filed in June, 2001 by the ACLU [American Civil Liberties Union] addressed some of these concerns at Locke High School in Los Angeles. Among the complaints were unreasonable searches, where students were frisked and spread-eagled and had their personal belongings examined in front of their peers. One of the plaintiffs in the case said "The searches are embarrassing. They're treating us like we're criminals. It's turning school into a prison." A former student told a reporter that "There are 27 cameras on the second floor alone and they are going to put up more cameras to supposedly make it a safer place, when really you feel more like a criminal." At Oswego High School in up-state New York, one such search was done without warning when several police squads with their drug-sniffing dogs searched students' lockers upon the request of the principal. They found a small amount of pot and a marijuana pipe in one student's pocket.

Perhaps the most infamous case occurred in a small town called Moose Creek, South Carolina. Videotape from surveillance cameras shows dozens of students, some of them handcuffed, sitting on a hallway floor against the walls as police officers watch them with guns drawn and police dogs sniff backpacks and bags strewn across the hall. A report in the *Los Angeles Times* noted that parents were outraged over the incident, saying that the police went overboard. No drugs were found. The author saw portions of the videotape and it looked like the *Gestapo* [Nazi secret police] with about 10 or 12 armed police roaming the halls yelling and making the students lie down on the floor.

Targeting Minor Offenders

Contrary to the media and most politicians, the most serious juvenile offenders—the so-called "chronic violent predator" or "super-predator"—are rare. All across the nation, we search in vain for these kinds of youths and discover that they usually constitute less than 3% of all juvenile offenders (but they

"Shall We Talk About Your Unacceptable Behavior or Shall We Go Directly to the Penalty Phase," cartoon by Aaron Bacall. CartoonStock.com.

dominate the headlines, making us think they are the norm). Upon the passage of various "get tough" laws, officials look in vain to find the "super-predators" and, finding few, end up targeting minor offenders. I call it the "trickle-down" effect.

Juvenile court statistics illustrate some of these trends. During the decade of the 1990s, referrals to juvenile court for serious crimes like robbery, aggravated assault, rape and homicide went down by more than 25%, while referrals for the category of "simple assault" went up by 128% (mostly fighting on school grounds or during domestic disturbances). While the most serious property crimes (e.g., burglary and motor vehicle theft) went down, drug offenses (mostly possession of pot) went up by 148%, while "obstruction of justice" and "disorderly conduct" both jumped up by 100%.

Sometimes we are told that a certain percentage of youths referred to juvenile court are charged with "crimes against the person" or "violent crimes" when in fact the majority of these crimes are rather minor in nature—a fist fight, a fight between children and their parents, between siblings, a mere threat, etc. In short, the kinds of personal confrontations that people of my generation used to get involved in all the time when we were young. What happened? The communities handled it—the schools, neighbors, community groups, and even the kids themselves. Even the police—like those where I grew up—handled these infractions through a stern lecture and a warning (chances are they knew you and/or your parents). How many adults recall being taken to juvenile court in handcuffs for wearing the wrong clothes or disrupting class?

Juvenile courts everywhere have become overworked with the huge caseloads of such minor offenses and many court officials have been complaining. In Toledo, the administrative judge for the Lucas County Juvenile Court said that we are "demonizing children," noting that in his court during the year 2002 there were 1,727 school-related cases, up from 1,237 in 2000 (a 40% increase). No doubt such cases increased again in 2003. The Toledo juvenile court's intake officer said that only about 2% of all school-related cases are serious incidents like students assaulting teachers. Similar complaints are heard all over the country. Marsha Levick, legal director for the Juvenile Law Center of Philadelphia, put the problem succinctly:

"The culture has shifted. Juvenile court is seen as an antidote for all sorts of behavior that in the past resulted in time out or suspension."

Discarding Children to the Juvenile Justice System

A critical factor in this recent trend is race. The majority of students charged with school-related offenses and ending up in juvenile court are minorities (in Toledo, 65% of the violators of the "safe school ordinance" have been minorities). This is nothing new, as it has become very clear that racism permeates the entire juvenile justice system, as recent juvenile court statistics reveal (e.g., blacks are far more likely to be detained and committed to a juvenile institution and are far more likely to he certified as an adult).

Racism is one aspect of this growing phenomenon. Another factor is the changing economic picture in American society, with increasing job losses, growing inequality, and more poverty, all of which place tremendous strains on people, with the inevitable strains on public services, including the juvenile court.

Sociologist Henry Giroux recently observed that there has been growing support in this country for the abandonment of young people, especially minorities, "to the dictates of a repressive penal state that increasingly addresses social problems through the police, courts, and prison system." This has been accomplished while the state has been increasingly reduced to providing police functions, at the expense of the role of serving as the "guardian of public interests." The policies of social investment, continues Giroux, "have given way to an emphasis on repression, surveillance, and control." One result is what he calls the "criminalization of social policy" or, perhaps more correctly, "domestic warfare."

A specific instance of this can be seen in New York City where, says Giroux, Rudi Giuliani [New York City mayor 1994–

2001] essentially assigned the role of discipline within the schools to the police department. In effect, the school principal has assumed the role of "warden" while many schools have added a new function: a "feeder system for the penal system" (Giroux, quoting Jesse Jackson [Baptist minister and civil rights activist]).

The war on terror and the war on Iraq, along with the expansion of American military might all over the globe, which is little more than another form of empire building and imperialism, is being matched by a growing crime control industry on the home front. Zero tolerance can be seen, therefore, as part of something much larger. My fear is that instituting anything remotely like radical nonintervention will be an uphill battle, given the current political climate. A "hands-off" policy toward youth does not fit in well these days, given the almost paranoid need to identify "troublemakers," "superpredators," and potential "terrorists."

> "It must be made absolutely clear that as part of any disciplinary policy that there are certain behaviors or offenses that are simply unacceptable in school settings under any circumstances."

Revised Zero Tolerance Laws Can Be Effective

American Psychological Association Zero Tolerance Task Force

In the following viewpoint, the American Psychological Association (APA) acknowledges the controversy surrounding zero tolerance policies in schools, but also maintains that schools must have a safe climate so that students can learn. To that end, the association suggests specific reforms that should be applied to zero tolerance policies, such as greater flexibility in handling infractions, reserving expulsion for only the most serious behaviors, and training on-campus police officers in adolescent develop-

This article is a reformatted and edited version of Russell Skiba, Cecil R. Reynolds, Sandra Graham, Peter Sheras, Jane Close Conoley, & Enedina Garcia-Vazquez, "Are Zero Tolerance Policies Effective in the Schools? An Evidentiary Review and Recommendations," A Report by the American Psychological Association Zero Tolerance Task Force, August 9, 2006. Copyright © 2006 by the American Psychological Association. Adapted with permission. The original Task Force Report is available at http://www.apa.org/ed/cpse/sttfreport.pdf. No further reproduction or distribution is permitted without the written permission of the American Psychological Association.

ment. The APA is the world's largest association of psychologists and works to advance psychology as a means of promoting health, education, and human welfare.

As you read, consider the following questions:

1. According to the American Psychological Association as cited in the viewpoint, what school employee should be the first person to contact parents or caregivers about a child's disciplinary problems at school?

2. Is it important to have carefully drawn definitions of behavioral infractions, or is it more appropriate to allow greater room for individual interpretation, according to the author?

3. Based on available data as cited by the APA, is there any racial disparity among students who are expelled from school?

The goal of any effective disciplinary system must be to ensure a safe school climate without threatening students' opportunity to learn. Zero tolerance has created controversy by threatening the opportunity to learn for great numbers of students. Moreover, our review of a large data base on school discipline reveals that, despite the removal of large numbers of purported troublemakers, zero tolerance policies have still not guaranteed safe school climates that ensure school learning. Clearly, an alternative course is necessary. . . .

By offering an evidence-based and comprehensive approach to school discipline, we hope the following recommendations will help schools and communities meet the critical goal of ensuring safe school climates conducive to learning without removing students from the opportunity to learn.

Greater Flexibility with Zero Tolerance Policies

Apply zero tolerance policies with greater flexibility, taking context and the expertise of teachers and school administrators into account. Allow teachers and other professional school staff who witness or encounter rule infractions common sense discretion in handling all but the most serious or serial infractions without making an office referral. Just as police officers have wide discretion in using their powers of citation and arrest, especially in the case of misdemeanor offenses, professional school staff on the scene of an infraction are often best equipped to appraise the circumstances and issues surrounding the rule infraction. Teachers and other professional staff who interact with students on a daily or weekly basis not only know the students best, but are the most likely school staff to have a relationship with the parents. This also means that administrators must clarify the expectation that teachers and other professional staff are expected to handle all but the most serious infractions or consistent, serial rule-breakers. Studies of effective principals suggest that they work with their teachers to define which of these offenses should be referred to the office, and which are better handled at the classroom level.

Teachers and other professional staff who have regular contact with students on a personal level should be the first line of communication with parents and caregivers regarding disciplinary incidents. Except in the case of the most egregious rule infractions by a student with no prior history of conduct problems, a school administrator such as a principal or member of the principal's staff should not be the first person to contact caregivers about disciplinary problems at school. Parents do not like surprises regarding children's problems and may react defensively and appropriately question why they were not consulted much earlier and given the opportunity to partner with the teacher and support staff in changing their child's behavior. It is to the benefit of all parties to avoid adverse relationships between parents and schools.

Fair and Equitable Behavior Management

Define all infractions, whether major or minor, carefully, and train all staff in appropriate means of handling each infraction. [Antoine] Garibaldi, [Loren] Blanchard, and [Steven] Brooks argued [in the 1996 article "Conflict Resolution Training, Teacher Effectiveness, and Student Suspension"] that inadequate reporting and definition allow greater room for individual bias to emerge in the disciplinary process. Carefully drawn definitions of all behaviors subject to the school disciplinary code protect both students from inequitable consequences, and school officials from charges of unfair and arbitrary application of school policy. Professional staff should be trained in multiple methods of behavior management. Classroom management should also be heavily infused into the curriculum of pre-service teachers as well, so that beginning teachers are prepared to handle the majority of misbehavior and minor disruption in their classroom, and to defuse rather than escalate behavioral incidents.

Evaluate all school discipline or school violence prevention strategies to ensure that all disciplinary interventions, programs, or strategies are truly impacting student behavior and school safety. Evaluate all school discipline policies to ensure that all intervention programs and strategies are implemented intelligently. The implementation of any procedure addressing student behavior or school violence—whether it be zero tolerance, conflict resolution, school security, or classroom management—must be accompanied by an evaluation adequate to determine whether that procedure has indeed made a positive contribution to improving school safety or student behavior. Without such data, there is the danger that time and resources will be wasted on strategies that sound appealing, but in fact do little to decrease a school's chances of disruption or violence. No intervention should be implemented without collecting data on its outcomes. Toward this end, increasing standardization and improvement in the technology of reporting and analyzing school disciplinary data will facilitate appropriate evaluation of disciplinary and violence prevention strategies.

A History of Zero Tolerance

The term *zero tolerance* was first employed by President Ronald Reagan's administration when it launched its War on Drugs initiative in the early 1980s. Some school districts embraced the initiative in an attempt to eradicate drug possession and drug use on school property. The policy became law, however, when Congress passed the Drug-Free Schools and Campuses Act of 1989 (Pub.L. 101-226, December 12, 1989, 103 Stat. 1928). The act banned the unlawful use, possession, or distribution of drugs and alcohol by students and employees on school grounds and college campuses. It required educational agencies and institutions of higher learning to establish disciplinary sanctions for violations or risk losing federal aid. As a result, the majority of schools and colleges immediately began to adopt zero tolerance polices to safeguard their federal funding.

Congress legislated zero tolerance polices toward weapons on school grounds when it passed the Gun-Free Schools Act of 1994 (Pub. L. 103-382, Title I, § 101, October 20, 1994, 198 Stat. 3907). According to the act, every state had to pass a law requiring educational agencies to expel from school, for not less than one year, any student found in possession of a gun. Students with disabilities under either the Individuals with Disabilities Act (IDEA) (Pub. L. 91-230, Title VI, April 13, 1970, 84 Stat. 175 to 188) or Section 504 of the Rehabilitation Act (Pub. L. 93-112, September 26, 1973, 87 Stat. 355) could be expelled for only 45 days. Despite these strict provisions, the act permitted school superintendents to modify the expulsion requirement on a case-by-case basis.

American Law Encyclopedia, Volume 10,
American Law and Legal Information,
"Zero Tolerance-Further Readings." http://law.jrank.org.

Graduated Systems of Discipline

Reserve zero tolerance disciplinary removals for only the most serious and severe of disruptive behaviors. Reserve expulsion for offenses that place other students or staff in jeopardy of physical or emotional harm. Federal courts have accepted arguments that the State's compelling interest in education is to prevent its citizens from becoming a burden on the State; students expelled from school have an increased probability of becoming such a burden through delinquency or incarceration. It is certainly appropriate to segregate repeat offenders from the general education population to preserve the safety of the school environment, but a focus on keeping students in an active learning environment, even in a separate facility if necessary, should be maintained.

Replace one-size-fits-all disciplinary strategies with graduated systems of discipline, wherein consequences are geared to the seriousness of the infraction. Provide teachers and other professional staff with a cascade of escalating options for discipline and a clear, common-sense method of making appropriate choices for applying discipline. In response to community concerns about punishments that do not fit the crime under zero tolerance, many school districts are implementing graduated systems of discipline, reserving severe punishment for only the most serious, safety-threatening offenses. Less serious offenses, such as classroom disruption, attendance related behaviors, or even minor fights among students are met with less severe consequences that might range from in-school suspension to parent contact, reprimands, community service, or counseling. It must be made absolutely clear as part of any disciplinary policy that there are certain behaviors or offenses that are simply unacceptable in school settings under any circumstances. Yet it is important to note that such an understanding does not in and of itself lead to a mandate of school removal for any specific offense. A comprehensive and effective disciplinary policy should specify both a continuum of possible actions and consequences, and provide guidance to school personnel regarding the permissible or recommended consequences for a given severity of behavior.

An Understanding of Adolescent Development

Require . . . police officers who work in schools to have training in adolescent development. For schools who have found a police presence to be valuable for preserving school safety, law enforcement approaches must be consistent with what we know about adolescent development. Adolescence is a time of positive and negative risk-taking that requires responsible adult guidance and support for positive decision making. Law enforcement strategies that stress punishment of offenders without understanding adolescent development run the risk of alienating youth from positive adults, thereby increasing the likelihood of maladaptive behavior. Thus, police officers in schools must be trained to understand that adolescent behavior must be carefully examined to ensure that minor, developmentally influenced misbehavior is not interpreted or treated like a criminal infraction. Further, examination of model disciplinary practices among principals suggests that effective programs involving police presence define the officer's role as proactively aiding the school in preventing student misbehavior through activities such as self-protection workshops, discussions of the function of law enforcement, and helping school teams in planning and executing crisis response plans.

Research Zero Tolerance Outcomes

Develop more systematic prospective studies on outcomes for children who are suspended or expelled from school due to zero tolerance policies. The evidence reviewed in this report suggests that the . . . outcomes [for individual children] associated with suspension and expulsion are of concern. Yet the field currently lacks individual, comprehensive longitudinal data measuring the direct and indirect effects of zero tolerance policies on school and life outcomes for individual students. Cross-sectional data provide rich descriptions of relationships at one point in time, but cannot show how relationships between policies and outcomes *develop* over time. It is possible, for example, that zero tolerance policies have a differential effect on students based on their prior history, current circumstances, influences of peer groups, or level of cognitive functioning. Further research is needed to describe how zero tolerance policies influence youth outcomes, to identify mechanisms through which district or state policy influences these outcomes, and to explore how characteristics of youth, families, and community might mediate these relationships.

Expand research on the connections between the education and juvenile justice systems, and in particular empirically test the support for a hypothesized school-to-prison pipeline. Evidence illustrating similarities between zero tolerance in the educational and juvenile justice systems, trends toward redefining school misbehavior as criminal infraction, the increased use of law enforcement for addressing school-based behavior, and the mandatory referral of certain offenses to law enforcement agencies all suggest that zero tolerance policies and suspension/expulsion may create, strengthen, or accelerate youth contact with the juvenile justice system. To date, however, linkages between school discipline and juvenile justice and the mechanisms through which they may influence each other have not been empirically tested. Prospective research that can explore the extent to which student disciplinary removal is related to increased likelihood of contact with juvenile justice systems is necessary in order to better understand to what extent and how these systems influence each other.

Racial, Disability Status, and Gender Disparities

Conduct research at the national level on disproportionate minority exclusion, or the extent to which school districts' use of zero tolerance disproportionately targets youth of color, particularly African American males. Based on available data, African American youth are two to three times more likely than White youth to be suspended or expelled for school infractions. Such disparities cannot be attributed to differences in socioeconomic status or to racial/ethnic differences in rates of misbehavior. As a first step toward developing action plans to remedy disproportionate minority exclusion, research is needed to systematically document whether particular school districts engage in zero tolerance policies that disproportionately target youth of color. This research would need to address contextual factors that could influence disproportionality, including the racial/ethnic composition of schools, geographic location, racial/ethnic background and training of the teaching staff, and presence of law enforcement personnel in the school. This review of the evidence suggests that African American youth are disciplined for less serious infractions or infractions that are based on a more subjective assessment of misbehavior. Further research is needed to explore the contribution of cultural stereotypes about race and antisocial behavior that may operate in as yet unspecified and perhaps unconscious ways.

Conduct research on disproportionate exclusion by disability status, specifically investigating the extent to which use of zero tolerance increases the disproportionate discipline of students with disabilities, and explore the extent to which differential rates of removal are due to intra-student factors versus system factors. Most available data suggests that students with disabilities, particularly students with ED [emotional disorders], are removed from school at rates higher than their proportion in the school enrollment. Reasons for these higher rates, however, are unclear. Future research should examine the extent to which higher rates of removal are due to social-behavioral shortcomings of students with disabilities (e.g. more frequent or serious misbehaviors), systems factors (e.g. differential perceptions of behaviors or administration of punishments by teachers and administrators, differential administration of zero tolerance policies) or some combination of the two. Research might also address the degree to which current disciplinary practice is consistent with the legal provisions governing the discipline of students with disabilities in IDEA [Individuals with Disabilities Education Act] 2004. Such research would necessitate attention to a host of contextual factors, such as rates of removal for students without disabilities, the extent of inclusion of students with disabilities, teacher use of effective classroom management strategies in general education settings, and the availability and use of resources specifically intended for students with disabilities.

Conduct research to enhance understanding of the potential differential effects of zero tolerance policies by student gender. While the evidence is consistent that males are overrepresented in school disciplinary indicators, reasons for such disproportionality, including the contribution of school and social contextual factors to gender differences, have not been widely explored to date. Future research should describe any changes in school disciplinary indicators by gender over time, to what degree these changes (if any) are related to changes in systems factors (e.g. zero tolerance) compared to intra-child behaviors (e.g. increases in violence), and to what degree evidence-based programs have a differential impact on by gender.

Benefits and Costs of Zero Tolerance Policies

Conduct econometric studies or cost-benefit analyses designed to explore the relative benefits of school removal for school climate as compared to the cost to society of removal of disciplined students from school. Removing students from school as a primary or sole intervention tool may have both potential benefits and costs to the school. While available evidence suggests that frequent student removal is associated with a host of negative outcomes, it is unclear what short-term benefits the school and society may gain by removing certain students from school. An empirical question to be addressed is the extent to which the potential benefits of zero tolerance outweigh the costs for schools and society in terms of student alienation, dropout, or juvenile incarceration. . . .

The accumulated evidence points to a clear need for change in how zero tolerance policies are applied, and toward the need for a set of alternative practices. These alternatives rely upon a more flexible and common-sense application of school discipline, and on a set of prevention practices that have been validated in ten years of school violence research. It is time to make the shifts in policy, practice, and research to implement policies that can keep schools safe *and* preserve the opportunity to learn for all students.

"*While some may criticize mandatory minimum penalties as unduly harsh, such penalties are invaluable tools to use against gangs.*"

Mandatory Minimum Sentences Will Reduce Youth Gang Violence

J. Randy Forbes

Congressman J. Randy Forbes, from the state of Virginia, professes in the following viewpoint that because gangs have become so violent and highly organized, severe measures must be taken to control their criminal activities. According to the U.S. Justice Department, over twenty-five thousand gangs are active in the United States. To protect citizens and communities from the increasing gang violence, Congressman Forbes is introducing the "Gang Deterrence and Community Protection Act of 2005" (H.R. 1279), which would require a mandatory minimum sentence of ten years in jail if convicted of committing a gang crime.

Editor's Note: H.R. 1279 passed in the House of Representatives, but failed in the Senate.

J. Randy Forbes, "Opening Statement of Congressman J. Randy Forbes, Legislative Hearing on H.R. 1279, 'The Gang Deterrence and Community Protection Act of 2005,'" judiciary.house.gov, April 5, 2005.

As you read, consider the following questions:

1. According to Forbes, what is the ratio of army and navy active duty personnel to gang members in the United States?

2. What do federal law-enforcement officers say they need from the local law-enforcement officers to combat the gang problem, according to the viewpoint?

3. What is the only effective means to ensure that fair and consistent sentences are imposed regarding gang members, according to Forbes?

Good morning. I want to welcome everyone to this important hearing to examine the issue of the problem of gang violence in America. The bill we are considering today sends a clear message to gangs: "It stops now."

Gone are the days of the "Sharks" and the "Jets" from The Westside Story [1957 musical about two teenage gangs in New York City]. No longer are fists and jeers the weapon of choice; now drive-by shootings with semi-automatics, brutal group beatings, and machete attacks are the standard. No longer are gangs loosely-knit groups or wayward teens. Today's criminal gangs are highly-organized, highly-structured bodies, whose ages range anywhere from elementary school to middle-age. They are trained in military techniques and their primary purpose is to commit illegal, violent criminal activities in furtherance of their gang organization. They are in our schools, on our streets, and in our communities. It stops now.

The Prevalence of Gangs

The problem of gangs is not a new one but a different one, and a bigger one, and one that is growing more rapidly and more uncontrollably than ever before. According to the U.S. Justice Department, there are currently over 25,000 gangs who are active in more than 3,000 jurisdictions across the United

States. Today the FBI and the U.S. Justice Department, estimate that there are somewhere between 750,000–850,000 gang members in our nation.

Let me put this in perspective for you: Today [2005], in our Army and Navy combined there are 859,000 active duty members. This is virtually a one-on-one ratio to gang members in the United States. You can even add the Air Force and the Marine Corps to that figure and we would not reach a 2 to 1 ratio of military personnel to criminal gang members. In fact, if the criminal gang members in the United States were a military force located in another country, they would comprise the 6th largest military in the world in terms of soldiers.

Gangs have declared war on our nation. They are ravaging our communities like cancer—urban, rural, rich and poor— and they are metastasizing from one community to the next as they grow. Today [2005], with the introduction of the "Gangbusters" legislation, we declare war on gangs. Our message to violent criminal gangs is this:

There is no overriding societal value to being a member of a gang and if you are a part of a gang we are coming at you twofold.

"Gangbuster" Legislation

First, this bill puts the full force of our nation's federal, state, and local law enforcement officers and prosecutors behind apprehending gangs. If you ask our nation's law enforcement officers what they need to combat gangs they will tell you this: Our federal law enforcement officers have the resources but not the intelligence system to combat the gang problem and our local law enforcement officers have the Intelligence network but not the resources to combat the problem. This bill will marry the two and authorize the funding to make this partnership successful.

Gangs, Drugs, and Guns

Despite the popular perception that belonging to a gang and drug-dealing go hand-in-hand, the research is somewhat contradictory. Recent studies conclude that larger gangs can be classified as "entrepreneurial gangs," that is, organized in a money-making enterprise like drug sales. Most gangs are better described as "street gangs," and are less focused on economic gain other than turf issues. Research conducted in California indicates that there was an increase in drug sales by gang members that paralleled high unemployment and the rise of the crack cocaine economy in the 1980s, but in general, drugs remain peripheral to the purposes and activities of the gang.

Even though most gang members are not involved in organized drug trafficking, concern over drugs and violence related to gangs is not unfounded. Studies show that young gang members have a higher drug usage rate than non-gang members. In addition, delinquency rates, including drug use, commission of violent offenses, and arrest rates, were higher for gang members.

Perhaps the most threatening aspect of gang proliferation has been the increasing use of firearms. Gang members are shown to possess significantly more guns than other at-risk youth. Studies cite "the threat of a rival gang," as the primary factor motivating youth to carry guns. Older youth and young adults are motivated more by the fact that their peers own guns, causing an escalating arms race of guns with greater and greater sophistication and lethality [in some communities].

National Youth Violence Prevention Resource Center,
"Gangs Fact Sheet," December 20, 2007. www.safeyouth.org.

Second, this bill says, that if you are a member of a gang and you commit a violent gang crime, you are going to jail for a minimum of ten years. Period.

While some may criticize mandatory-minimum penalties as unduly harsh, such penalties are invaluable tools to use against gangs to secure cooperation from gang members and infiltrate tightly-knit organized crime syndicates operating as sophisticated street gangs. Moreover, in light of the Supreme Court's recent [2005] decision in *[United States vs.] Booker* and *[United States vs.] Fanfan* rendering the guidelines as only advisory, mandatory minimums are the only effective means to ensure that fair and consistent sentences are imposed, and we will see more of them unless something is done to re-impose a mandatory guideline system.

This bill will create new criminal gang prosecution offenses, enhance existing violent crime penalties to deter and punish criminal gangs, and enact violent crime reforms needed to effectively prosecute gang members. This is a tough bill. We're not playing around. We are saying that the following is not acceptable in America:

- Gangs that fuel their activity with narcotics trafficking, carjacking, and illegal gun trafficking

- Gangs that engage in human trafficking, rape, and prostitution

- Gangs that use firearms and other deadly weapons in the commission of crimes

- Gangs that brutally rape, kill, and maim

The Gangbusters Bill, when enacted, will bring a new force to bear on gang activity in our country. It will provide increased federal effort to assist local law enforcement in targeting and federally prosecuting violent criminals who are associated with street gangs. The bill will encourage partnerships across all levels of government and ensure the success of these partnerships through the expansion of resources and intelligence.

> *"Mandatory minimums result in unwarranted sentencing disparities. They treat dissimilar offenders in a similar manner although those offenders can be quite different with respect to the seriousness of their conduct or their danger to society."*

Mandatory Minimum Sentences Will Not Reduce Youth Gang Violence

Robert C. Scott

In the following viewpoint, Robert C. Scott maintains that mandatory minimum sentences are counterproductive in the fight against youth crime. Studies have shown that juveniles go on to commit even more violent crimes once they are released from prison. Furthermore, according to the Judicial Conference of the United States, the imposition of identical sentences on dissimilar offenders is unreasonable and unjust. Scott suggests that the United States use the taxpayers' dollars on crime prevention and intervention programs rather than on jail cells for juvenile offenders. Robert C. Scott is a U.S. congressman from the state of Virginia.

Robert C. Scott, "Hearing Before the Subcommittee on Crime, Terrorism, and Homeland Security of the Committee on the Judiciary House of Representatives," judiciary.house.gov, April 5, 2005.

Editor's Note: H.R. 1279, The Gang Deterrence and Community Protection Act of 2005, passed in the House of Representatives, but failed in the Senate.

As you read, consider the following questions:

1. According to the U.S. Sentencing Commission as mentioned in the viewpoint, are minorities more or less likely to receive mandatory minimum sentences under comparable circumstances?

2. How does the U.S. prison population compare per capita with that of the rest of the world, according to the author?

3. What are two reasons that kids join gangs, according to students from Monument High School in South Boston, Massachusetts, as cited in the viewpoint?

This bill [H.R. 1279, The Gang Deterrence and Protection Act of 2005] is chock-full of new mandatory minimum sentences, ranging from a mandatory minimum of 10 years to mandatory life or death and other provisions, which have been solidly proven to be counterproductive in the fight against crime. They are not criticized because they are harsh. They are criticized because they are counterproductive. We have known that mandatory minimum sentences disrupt order and proportionality in sentencing. They discriminate against minorities and waste taxpayers' money, compared to sentencing schemes where the court can look at the seriousness of the crime and the offender's role in the crime and background.

Minimum Sentences: "More Harm than Good"

The Judicial Conference of the United States, which sees the impact of mandatory minimum sentences on individual cases, as well as the criminal justice system as a whole, has told us

Investing in Children, Not Prisons

Successful strategies to combat youth violence and gang-related activity have long eluded lawmakers who too often rely on enacting longer sentences for young people instead of implementing proven prevention and intervention programs that stop violence before it happens. . . .

Children are our most precious resource and by providing the care and services they need while they are young we can improve their chances for success. Neighborhoods confronted with juvenile crime will be better served by keeping children in school rather than locking them behind bars. According to data from 1999, over 40% of young black males without a high school diploma were in prison or jail. Among young white male dropouts, one out of 10 was incarcerated. These stark statistics serve as a warning sign that efforts to stop crime must start early and include a comprehensive strategy for a child's success.

Marc Mauer,
Executive Director,
The Sentencing Project.

time and time again that mandatory minimum sentences create more harm than good from any kind of rational evaluation. In its recent letter to Members of the Subcommittee on Crime regarding this bill, the Conference noted that mandatory minimum sentences create, quote, "the opposite of their intended effect." Continuing to quote, "Far from fostering certainty in punishment, mandatory minimums result in unwarranted sentencing disparities. They treat dissimilar offenders in a similar manner although those offenders can be quite different with respect to the seriousness of their conduct or their danger to society." And they finally say that "they require the sentencing court to impose the same sentence on offenders when sound policy and common sense call for reasonable differences in punishment."

Both the Federal Judicial Center in its report entitled, "The General Effects of Mandatory Minimum Prison Terms: A Longitudinal Study of Federal Sentences Imposed," and the United States Sentencing Commission in its study entitled, "Mandatory Minimum Penalties in the Federal Criminal Justice System," found that minorities were substantially more likely than whites under comparable circumstances to receive mandatory minimum sentences. A Rand Corporation study entitled, "Mandatory Drug Sentences: Throwing Away the Key or the Taxpayers' Money?" showed that mandatory minimum sentences are far less effective than either discretionary sentences or drug treatment in reducing drug-related crime and, thus, far costlier than either.

Just how costly this bill will be is yet to be seen, but, in response to an inquiry by my office, the U.S. Sentencing Commission estimated that the prison impact of H.R 1279 would require an additional 23,600 prison beds over the next 10 years. At $75,000 a cell, that amounts to prison construction costs of almost $2 billion, in addition to annual upkeep of about $750 million based on $30,000 per inmate per year. That is over and above what we are already scheduled to spend on prison construction and prison inkeep in a country where the prison population per person is higher than anywhere else in the world. For proven juvenile crime prevention and intervention programs, we are spending about half, about $400 million, of the annual inmate upkeep this bill will cost.

Juveniles Tried as Adults

The worst problem with this bill is it provides for far more juveniles being tried as adults. For years now, every study of juveniles tried as adults has shown that juveniles commit more crimes, more violent crimes in particular, when they are released, if they are treated as adults. This is easy to understand when you consider that juveniles who go to prison will have as their role models hardcore murderers, rapists, and robbers, whereas in the juvenile detention system they will receive education and training, counseling, drug treatment, and other assistance.

On March 14 of this year [2005], coincidentally the same day that H.R. 1279 was introduced, the Coalition for Juvenile Justice released its study, "Childhood on Trial: The Failure of Trying and Sentencing Youth in Adult Criminal Court," showed even more definitively that trying juveniles as adults increased rather than decreased the prospects that they would reoffend when released and that with more serious offenses, as compared with the youth tried in juvenile court. The study revealed that over 250,000 youth are charged as adults every year. Just as with the application of mandatory minimums, the application of adult court to juveniles falls heaviest amongst minorities, about 82 percent of youths tried as adults are youth of color.

Prevention Programs Instead of Minimum Sentences

For years, we have known that a continuum of services geared toward the needs of at-risk youths prevents crime from occurring in the first place. Many such proven crime prevention programs have saved more money than they cost. Head Start and other quality early childhood education programs, Boys and Girls Clubs, and after-school recreational programs, Job Corps and other intensive job training programs, all prevent crime and save more money than they cost.

At a meeting I had with students at Monument High School in South Boston, Massachusetts, last month [March 2005], I told them about this upcoming hearing and asked them what was needed to prevent gang crime. They said kids join gangs for reputation, protection, to feel wanted, to have friends, and to get money, and what is needed to prevent them from joining gangs was ample recreation for boys as well as girls, jobs and internships for training and money, and assistance to allow their families to live in a decent home.

Interestingly, I asked the same question to a group of law enforcement officials I met in my district yesterday, and they had very similar advice. Neither group said anything about the need for more mandatory minimums or trying more juveniles as adults.

So we know what works to prevent crime. Unfortunately, we also know how to play politics. H.R. 1279 has been nicknamed "Gangbusters." It reflects the politics of crimes where you come up with a good slogan and try to codify it. It doesn't matter whether it does anything to reduce crime or is counterproductive, but, if it sounds good, it must work.

We have had the greatest success by putting aside the politics of crime in favor of sound policy in the area of juvenile justice, until this bill. Three years ago, we passed a bipartisan juvenile crime prevention and bipartisan juvenile early intervention bill. These bills were based on the advice of judges, administrators, researchers, advocates, and law enforcement officials, representing the entire political spectrum. They all said the same thing, that the best way to reduce and prevent juvenile crime and ultimately adult crime is through prevention and early intervention programs geared at at-risk youth. None of them said that we need more mandatory minimum sentences nor that we need to treat more juveniles as adults.

Both bills passed virtually unanimously in both the House and the Senate, and yet the funding in these bills has been cut in half since they passed, including the gang resistance funding, and now we wonder why we have increases in gang violence after we've cut all the funds to prevent it. We must get back to the bipartisan, evidence-based, universally agreed-upon approach to preventing juvenile crime and gang violence and abandon the sound bite-based, politically-charged approaches which cost billions of dollars and actually increased crime and violence.

Periodical Bibliography

The following articles have been selected to supplement the diverse views presented in this chapter.

Afterschool Alliance — "Afterschool Programs: Keeping Kids—and Communities—Safe," afterschoolalliance.org, April 2007.

Anne Blythe — "When Should Teens Be Tried as Adults?" *(North Carolina) News & Observer*, June 17, 2007.

Marian Wright Edelman — "We Must Stem Gun Violence," Childrensdefense.org, 2007.

Adam Geller — "Juveniles Do Hard Time for Harsh Crimes," *USA Today*, December 9, 2007.

David E. Graham — "His Goal: Get Kids Away from Gangs," *San Diego Union Tribune*, December 31, 2007.

Janine Kearney — "Drugs, Mental Illness, Abuse Contribute to Teen Crime," *Daily Sparks Tribune*, 2007.

Mary Beth Lane — "Serious Offenders: Youths Can Get One Last Chance," *Columbus Dispatch*, January 11, 2008.

Cathy Lanier and Vincent Schiraldi — "Give Us Back Our Gun Law," *Washington Post*, March 15, 2007.

Terry A. Maroney — "Should Juveniles Be Tried as Adults?" *The Tennessean*, January 8, 2007.

Newsweek.com — "When Children Kill: America Has Toughened Up on Kids Who Murder and Commit Other Crimes. Is It Working?" December 17, 2007.

Will Okun — "Our Own?" *New York Times*, October 31, 2007.

Sharon Smith — "Zero Tolerance Means Jail for Minority Youth," SocialistWorker.org, April 20, 2007.

OPPOSING VIEWPOINTS® SERIES

CHAPTER 4

How Can Teen Substance Abuse Be Reduced?

Chapter Preface

Tobacco use is the number one preventable cause of death in America. Every day approximately four thousand kids will smoke a cigarette for the first time, according to William V. Corr, executive director of the Campaign for Tobacco-Free Kids. Another one thousand will become regular smokers, one-third of whom will die prematurely. "Tobacco use," said the U.S. Supreme Court in 2002, "particularly among children and adolescents, poses perhaps the single most significant threat to public health in the United States." Because tobacco products today contain more than sixty cancer-causing substances, the National Cancer Institute claims that disease among smokers has actually increased despite the 1964 Surgeon General's warning about tobacco's health risks. The end result is that many state senators, representatives, public health organizations, and close to 77 percent of American registered voters want the tobacco industry to be regulated by the federal government.

Attempts at federal regulation over the tobacco industry have struggled for decades with no success. With the 1998 Master Settlement Agreement, in which tobacco companies agreed to restrict advertising and marketing to young people and to fund antismoking campaigns, many health organizations hoped the nation's teenage smoking rate would lower dramatically. Instead, some claim, by spending over $13 billion each year, tobacco companies have continued to surreptitiously market their products in ways that appeal to children—such as flavored cigarettes and smokeless tobacco—and kids continue to use tobacco at alarmingly high rates. As an example of the effects of advertising aimed at children, smokeless tobacco was popular primarily with older men in the past; now it is used predominately by young boys. In response to what many call the tobacco industry's bad faith behavior,

Senator Edward M. Kennedy of Massachusetts has introduced legislation that would give the U.S. Food and Drug Administration (FDA) authority to oversee the manufacture, marketing, and sale of tobacco products for health and safety purposes.

Among other provisions, the legislation would enable the FDA to effectively ban marketing practices that target teens, such as promoting candy-flavored smokeless tobacco, and advertising in magazines with high youth readerships. Additionally, the FDA could restrict the tobacco industry's deceptive claims that tobacco products with reduced tar and nicotine are safe or less risky; scientific evidence has shown that "light" and "low tar" products do not reduce the risk of disease. Furthermore, the proposed legislation would give the FDA authority to require the removal of harmful, addictive ingredients or to mandate a reduction in nicotine levels in tobacco products.

Those in health professions, youth advocacy groups, and the general public believe that federal regulation of the tobacco industry is necessary and long overdue. As Senator Kennedy remarked, "We have a real opportunity to save a generation of Americans from a lifetime of addiction and certain death." Authors in the following chapter further discuss solutions to reduce tobacco use and other substance abuse among teenagers.

> "American society has determined that upon turning 18 teenagers become adults."

The Minimum Legal Drinking Age Should Be Lowered

Choose Responsibility

The authors at Choose Responsibility, a nonprofit organization founded in 2007, discuss in the following viewpoint several issues concerning the debate over lowering the legal drinking age from twenty-one to eighteen. For example, the authors point out that eighteen-year-olds in America are legally allowed to buy cigarettes, purchase property, vote, and serve on a jury—yet are not legally allowed to purchase or drink alcoholic beverages. The organization also maintains that education programs about using alcohol safely are effective at reducing high-risk drinking.

As you read, consider the following questions:

1. According to Choose Responsibility, at what age do Americans become legally responsible for their actions?
2. Alcohol education programs can generally be grouped into what two categories, according to the organization?

"Debating the Issues," 2007, chooseresponsibility.org, 2007. Reproduced by permission.

3. Does H.S. Swartzwelder believe that the brain of an adolescent has finished developing by the age of eighteen?

D ebating the Issues . . .

- If a person can go to war, shouldn't he or she be able to have a beer?

- Many youth under age 21 still drink, despite the current legal drinking age. Doesn't that prove the policy is ineffective?

- Youth in other countries are exposed to alcohol at earlier ages and engage in less alcohol abuse and have healthier attitudes toward alcohol. Don't those countries have fewer alcohol-related problems than we do?

- I've read that if we educate teens about using alcohol safely starting at age 18, that will encourage responsible drinking. Is that true?

- I've read that the adolescent brain continues to develop through the early 20s. What are the long-term effects of alcohol use on a developing brain?

- There seems to be support for lowering the drinking age—is this true?

- So what strategies are effective for reducing high-risk alcohol use?. . .

Old Enough for War, Old Enough for Alcohol

For better or worse, American society has determined that upon turning 18 teenagers become adults. This means they can enlist [in the military], serve, fight and potentially die for their country. And while the "fight for your country" argument is a powerful one, it only begins to capture the essence of adulthood. Most importantly, at age 18 you become legally responsible for your actions. You can buy and smoke cigarettes even though you know that, in time, they will probably give you lung cancer. You may even purchase property, strike binding legal contracts, take out a loan, vote, hold office, serve on a jury, or adopt a child. But strangely at 18, one cannot buy a beer. While that may be an injustice to those choosing to serve their country, the more serious consequence is the postponement of legal culpability. In most other countries, the age of majority coincides with the legal drinking or purchasing age.

Critics are quick to point out that 18 is not an age of majority, but one step amongst many that together mark the gradual path to adulthood. This argument notes that young adults cannot drink until 21, rent cars until 25, run for the U.S. Senate until they are 30, and run for President until 35. This is, the critics suggest, evidence of a graduated legal adulthood. But this argument falls flat. First, rental car companies are not legally prevented from renting cars to those under 25; this is a decision made by insurance companies. In fact, some rental companies do rent to those under 25, and the associated higher rates compensate for that potential liability. Second, age requirements for these high public offices are more appropriately seen as exceptions to full adulthood, rather than benchmarks of adulthood. Finally, and most importantly, the Constitution speaks to the legal age of majority only once and that is in the 26th Amendment to the Constitution where, "The right of citizens of the US, who are 18 years of age or older, to vote shall not be denied or abridged . . . on account of age.". . .

Minors Drink Alcohol Despite Policies

Many young people under the age of 21 consume alcohol, and continue to do so despite nearly 25 years worth of prohibition of that behavior. The trend over the past decade has had a polarizing effect of sorts—fewer 12–20-year-olds are drinking, but those who choose to drink are drinking more. Between 1993 and 2001, the rate of 12–20-year-olds who reported consuming alcohol in the past 30 days decreased from 33.4% to 29.3%, while rates of binge drinking increased among that age group over those same years, from 15.2% to 18.9%. Data specific to college and university students also indicate this polarization of drinking behaviors over time. A decade's worth of research in the College Alcohol Study found both the proportion of students abstaining and the proportion of students engaging in frequent binge drinking had increased. Furthermore, as compared to 1993, more 18–24-year-old students who chose to drink in 2001 were drinking excessively—defined by frequency of drinking occasions, frequency of drunkenness, and drinking to get drunk.

There is evidence that the decline in alcohol consumption by those under the age of 21 seen throughout the 1980s and 1990s was not the result of the 21-year-old drinking age, but of a larger societal trend. "Nationwide per capita consumption peaked around 1980 and dropped steeply during the 1980s. Drinking by youths followed this same pattern. The predominant reason was not changes in state MLDA [minimum legal drinking age] but rather a close link between youthful and adult alcohol consumption. . . . Increasing the MLDA did make some difference but not as much as might be guessed from a simple 'before and after' comparison." Even the 1993 source so frequently cited in support of the 21-year-old drinking age acknowledges that ". . . [survey-based research from the 1970s] has shown that increased minimum age both does and does not covary with decreased youth drinking." This evidence suggests that the 21-year-old drinking age is not an unqualified success, but rather a well-intentioned social policy whose 25-year history has led to several unintended consequences, including but not limited to an increase in the prevalence of abusive drinking amongst young people. . . .

Europeans Drink Alcohol at Younger Ages

Any generalizations of the behavior of "European" youth should be scrutinized. The drinking cultures of northern and southern European nations vary markedly; history and an extensive body of cross cultural research would suggest that cultural attitudes towards alcohol use play a far more influential role than minimum age legislation. Recent research published by the World Health Organization found that while 15- and 16-year-old teens in many European states, where the drinking age is 18 or younger (and often unenforced), have more drinking occasions per month, they have fewer dangerous, intoxication occasions than their American counterparts. For example, in southern European nations ratios of all drinking occasions to intoxication occasions were quite low—roughly one in ten—while in the United States, almost half of all drinking occasions involving 15- and 16-year-olds resulted in intoxication.

Though its legal drinking age is highest among all the countries surveyed, the United States has a higher rate of dangerous intoxication occasions than many countries that not only have drinking ages that are lower or nonexistent, but also have much higher levels of per capita consumption.

Research also notes that the 15- and 16-year-olds who are most at risk for alcohol problems (defined as those who consume alcohol 10 times or more in 30 days and drink to intoxication three times or more in 30 days) are not those who live in countries where overall per capita consumption is highest, but rather from the countries where it is lower. For example, though France and Portugal have the highest per capita consumption in Europe, 15- and 16-year-olds in both countries show very moderate consumption. By contrast, Denmark, Ireland, and the United Kingdom, where per capita consumption is comparatively low, have the highest number of at-risk 15- and 16-year-olds. Per capita consumption and the degree of risk for serious alcohol problems, therefore, are inversely proportional. . . .

Alcohol Education Courses Teach Responsible Drinking

The effectiveness of alcohol education continues to be widely debated. Various approaches to alcohol education have been developed and can generally be grouped into those that support abstinence and those that view abstinence as unrealistic, and must therefore work to equip individuals with decision-making skills for safe alcohol use. There are both formal education, through schools and institutions, and informal education through the family and peers. While alcohol education programs that advocate abstinence have been proven ineffective, interactive education programs have had greater success in their ability not only to educate drinkers, but also to alter their drinking habits.

Australia has successfully implemented alcohol education programs that focus on reducing risk and promoting responsible drinking. *Rethinking Drinking*, and its counterpart aimed at a younger crowd, *School Health and Alcohol Harm Reduction Project*, include role playing and interactive teaching and build skills so students may safely handle risky situations involving alcohol. These programs have shown some effectiveness in influencing young adults' drinking behaviors.

Recently in the United States, *Outside the Classroom* has produced *AlcoholEDU*, an interactive online prevention program used by 450 colleges and universities throughout the country. *AlcoholEDU* increases practical knowledge, motivates students to change their behavior, and decreases students' risk of negative personal and academic consequences as a result of alcohol use. In 2004, students who completed *AlcoholEDU* were 20% less likely to be heavy-episodic drinkers and 30%

The History of the Minimum Legal Drinking Age of 21

On April 14, 1982, President [Ronald] Reagan established the Presidential Commission Against Drunk Driving (PCDD). This commission established 39 recommendations to curb what was perceived to be a drunken driving epidemic. Taken together, the 39 recommendations were intended to be a comprehensive approach with a goal of reducing the number of alcohol-related deaths on the nation's highways. Recommendation number eight concerned the Minimum Legal Purchasing Age, and said that all states should raise the Minimum Legal Drinking Age (MLDA) to 21, lest they lose a certain percentage of federal highway dollars. Though the target of the Commission's recommendations was intended to be drunk driving across the adult population, the disproportionate amount of attention paid to establishing 21 as the national minimum drinking age shifted the nation's focus to young people's drinking. Exclusive interest in raising the drinking age marginalized the effect of the remaining 38 recommendations, among them suggestions to implement youth education programs, establish a massive public information campaign, and to increase penalties for convicted drunken drivers. Two years later, on July 17, 1984, after extensive lobbying from groups such as MADD [Mothers Against Drunk Driving], President Reagan signed the National Minimum Drinking Age Act, effectively creating a national minimum drinking age of 21. By 1987, all 50 states had legislated Legal Age 21.

Choose Responsibility, 2007.

less likely to be problematic drinkers, numbers that prove that alcohol education can be a useful tool in altering students' drinking habits.

Upon finding a lack of thorough research regarding the effects of alcohol education, Andrew F. Wall, Ph.D., of the University of Illinois at Urbana-Champaign began his study of the effectiveness of *AlcoholEDU*. He describes his research as aiming to "determine whether an online prevention program would change behavior and consequences." His research provides evidence for the first time that ". . . an interactive educational experience can substantially reduce the negative consequences of high-risk drinking.". . .

The Manner in Which Alcohol Affects a Teen's Brain

[Author's Note:] *We asked Dr. H.S. Swartzwelder, frequently cited expert on adolescent brain development and substance abuse, MADD [Mothers Against Drunk Driving] consultant, and Choose Responsibility board member to respond to this question.*

"It is true that the brain continues to develop into a person's 20s, particularly the frontal lobes which are critical for many of the higher cognitive functions that are so important for success in the adult world—such as problem solving, mental flexibility, and planning.

"It is also clear that alcohol affects the adolescent brain differently than the adult brain, but the story is not simple and the data should be interpreted cautiously as this complex science continues to evolve. Although alcohol affects some brain functions more powerfully during adolescence, it affects other functions less powerfully during the same period. For example, studies in animals clearly indicate that a single dose of alcohol can impair learning (and learning-related brain activity) more powerfully in adolescent animals than in adults. But on the other hand a somewhat higher dose will produce far greater sedation (and sedation-related brain activity) in adult animals than in adolescents. So, in terms of single doses of alcohol, the adolescent brain is not uniformly more or less sensitive to alcohol—it depends on the brain function that is being measured. Importantly, there has been little direct study of the effects of acute doses of alcohol on adolescent humans, compared to adults. One study found that a single dose of alcohol resulting in blood alcohol levels near 80mg/dl (the legal limit) impaired learning more powerfully among people in their early 20s than it did in people in their late 20s, but it will take more research to answer this question with authority in human subjects.

"Since the effects of single doses of alcohol can have markedly different effects on adolescents than on adults, it makes sense to ask whether this means that the adolescent brain is more or less sensitive to the effects of repeated doses of alcohol over time. In my view, the jury remains out on this question, but there are some studies in animals which suggest that the adolescent brain may be more vulnerable to long-term damage by alcohol than the adult brain. Similarly, there are some studies of humans who consumed large quantities of alcohol over extended periods of time during adolescence, and have relatively small hippocampi (a brain region critical for certain types of learning). All of these studies need to be fleshed out before the issue is settled, but, if nothing else, they give teens a very good reason to think carefully about drinking to excess . . . and this is probably the pivotal issue—how much is too much?

"Most studies of the effects of chronic alcohol exposure in adolescence, compared to adulthood, have focused on relatively high doses. Studies of lower doses, and less severe chronic dosing regimens, will be needed to determine whether the adolescent brain is more sensitive to the long-term effects of mild to moderate drinking. There are plenty of studies indicating that early, unsupervised drinking can lead to trouble for teens—both immediately and down the road. But this does not mean that an 18-year-old who has a beer or two every couple of weeks is doing irreparable damage to her brain.

It is the 18-year-old (or 30-year old, for that matter!) who downs five or six drinks in a row on his way to a dance that worries me." . . .

Support Exists for Lowering the Drinking Age

There is support for lowering the drinking age, though polling data suggests this remains a minority view. Since the Supreme Court decision in *South Dakota v. Dole* in 1987, however (South Dakota, joined by the states of Colorado, Hawaii, Kansas, Louisiana, Montana, New Mexico, Ohio, South Carolina, Tennessee, Vermont, and Wyoming had challenged the constitutionality of the 1984 legislation), there has been virtually no public discussion or debate over the 21-year-old drinking age. Twenty years have passed, during which time data have been gathered and the practical effects of the law have been experienced. National (*Chronicle of Higher Education*; *US News and World Report*; *Newsweek*; Fox News) media interest in the issue, perhaps or perhaps not reflecting a change in public opinion, has surfaced repeatedly during the first half of 2007. This would suggest a desire to reopen debate. . . .

Certain Approaches Are Effective in Reducing High-Risk Alcohol Use

Strategies based on harm reduction and environmental management have been successful in reducing underage alcohol abuse. While research has shown that abstinence-based education programs alone have little to no effect on preventing use or abuse of alcohol among underage drinkers, harm reduction strategies that address the complex psychological expectancies that lead to excessive drinking amongst young people are effective in reducing rates and incidences of alcohol abuse. Environmental strategies such as alcohol advertising bans, keg registration, responsible server training, social norms marketing and community interventions are viable options for managing high-risk drinking, especially on college campuses. Furthermore, evidence would suggest that a policy based on strengthening enforcement may be of limited success; for every 1,000 incidences of underage alcohol consumption, only two result in arrest or citation. Advocates of enforcement should be required to demonstrate the level of incremental expense they would recommend in order to achieve a significantly better result. Under the 21-year-old drinking age, fewer underage individuals are drinking, but those who do choose to drink are drinking more, are drinking in ways that are harmful to their health, and [are] engaging in behaviors that have a negative impact on the community.

"Increasing the age at which people can legally purchase and drink alcohol has been the most successful intervention to date in reducing drinking and alcohol-related crashes among people under age 21."

The Minimum Legal Drinking Age Should Not Be Lowered

U.S. Department of Health and Human Services

In the following viewpoint, the U.S. Department of Health and Human Services (DHHS) breaks down the risks of alcohol consumption of young people under the age of 21. This viewpoint contends that the most successful way to prevent underage drinking is to keep the legal drinking age at 21. HHS estimates this minimum saves about 700 to 1,000 lives annually. HHS is the United States government's principal agency for protecting the health of all Americans and providing essential human services, especially for those who are least able to help themselves

As you read, consider the following questions:

1. What was the average age of first use by adolescents in 2003, as stated in the viewpoint?

U.S. Department of Health and Human Services, "Underage Drinking: Why Do Adolescents Drink, What are the Risks, and How Can Underage Drinking Be Prevented?" January 2006. Reproduced by permission.

2. According to the authors, what are some of the health risks of adolescent drinking?

3. What did the New Zealand study show about how much the legal drinking age relates to drinking-related crashes?

Alcohol is the drug of choice among youth. Many young people are experiencing the consequences of drinking too much, at too early an age. As a result, underage drinking is a leading public health problem in this country.

Each year, approximately 5,000 young people under the age of 21 die as a result of underage drinking; this includes about 1,900 deaths from motor vehicle crashes, 1,600 as a result of homicides, 300 from suicide, as well as hundreds from other injuries such as falls, burns, and drownings.

Yet drinking continues to be widespread among adolescents, as shown by nationwide surveys as well as studies in smaller populations. According to data from the 2005 Monitoring the Future (MTF) study, an annual survey of U.S. youth, three-fourths of 12th graders, more than two-thirds of 10th graders, and about two in every five 8th graders have consumed alcohol. And when youth drink they tend to drink intensively, often consuming four to five drinks at one time. MTF data show that 11 percent of 8th graders, 22 percent of 10th graders, and 29 percent of 12th graders had engaged in heavy episodic (or "binge") drinking within the past two weeks.

Research also shows that many adolescents start to drink at very young ages. In 2003, the average age of first use of alcohol was about 14, compared to about 17 1/2 in 1965. People who reported starting to drink before the age of 15 were four times more likely to also report meeting the criteria for alcohol dependence at some point in their lives. In fact, new research shows that the serious drinking problems (including what is called alcoholism) typically associated with middle age actually begin to appear much earlier, during young adulthood and even adolescence.

Other research shows that the younger children and adolescents are when they start to drink, the more likely they will be to engage in behaviors that harm themselves and others. For example, frequent binge drinkers (nearly 1 million high school students nationwide) are more likely to engage in risky behaviors, including using other drugs such as marijuana and cocaine, having sex with six or more partners, and earning grades that are mostly Ds and Fs in school.

Why Some Adolescents Drink

As children move from adolescence to young adulthood, they encounter dramatic physical, emotional, and lifestyle changes. Developmental transitions, such as puberty and increasing independence, have been associated with alcohol use. So in a sense, just being an adolescent may be a key risk factor not only for starting to drink but also for drinking dangerously.

Research shows the brain keeps developing well into the twenties, during which time it continues to establish important communication connections and further refines its function. Scientists believe that this lengthy developmental period may help explain some of the behavior which is characteristic of adolescence—such as their propensity to seek out new and potentially dangerous situations. For some teens, thrill-seeking might include experimenting with alcohol. Developmental changes also offer a possible physiological explanation for why teens act so impulsively, often not recognizing that their actions—such as drinking—have consequences.

How people view alcohol and its effects also influences their drinking behavior, including whether they begin to drink and how much. An adolescent who expects drinking to be a pleasurable experience is more likely to drink than one who does not. An important area of alcohol research is focusing on how expectancy influences drinking patterns from childhood through adolescence and into young adulthood. Beliefs about alcohol are established very early in life, even before the child begins elementary school. Before age 9, children generally view alcohol negatively and see drinking as bad, with adverse effects. By about age 13, however, their expectancies shift, becoming more positive. As would be expected, adolescents who drink the most also place the greatest emphasis on the positive and arousing effects of alcohol.

Differences between the adult brain and the brain of the maturing adolescent also may help to explain why many young drinkers are able to consume much larger amounts of alcohol than adults before experiencing the negative consequences of drinking, such as drowsiness, lack of coordination, and withdrawal/hangover effects. This unusual tolerance may help to explain the high rates of binge drinking among young adults. At the same time, adolescents appear to be particularly sensitive to the positive effects of drinking, such as feeling more at ease in social situations, and young people may drink more than adults because of these positive social experiences.

Pinpointing a genetic contribution will not tell the whole story, however, as drinking behavior reflects a complex interplay between inherited and environmental factors, the implications of which are only beginning to be explored in adolescents. And what influences drinking at one age may not have the same impact at another. As Rose and colleagues show, genetic factors appear to have more influence on adolescent drinking behavior in late adolescence than in mid-adolescence.

Environmental factors, such as the influence of parents and peers, also play a role in alcohol use. For example, parents who drink more and who view drinking favorably may have children who drink more, and an adolescent girl with an older or adult boyfriend is more likely to use alcohol and other drugs and to engage in delinquent behaviors.

Researchers are examining other environmental influences as well, such as the impact of the media. Today alcohol is widely available and aggressively promoted through television, radio, billboards, and the Internet. Researchers are studying how young people react to these advertisements. In a study of 3rd, 6th, and 9th graders, those who found alcohol ads desirable were more likely to view drinking positively and to want to purchase products with alcohol logos. Research is mixed, however, on whether these positive views of alcohol actually lead to underage drinking.

Health Risks

Whatever it is that leads adolescents to begin drinking, once they start they face a number of potential health risks. Although the severe health problems associated with harmful alcohol use are not as common in adolescents as they are in adults, studies show that young people who drink heavily may put themselves at risk for a range of potential health problems.

Scientists currently are examining just how alcohol affects the developing brain, but it's a difficult task. Subtle changes in the brain may be difficult to detect but still have a significant impact on long-term thinking and memory skills. Add to this the fact that adolescent brains are still maturing, and the study of alcohol's effects becomes even more complex. Research has shown that animals fed alcohol during this critical developmental stage continue to show long-lasting impairment from alcohol as they age. It's simply not known how alcohol will affect the long-term memory and learning skills of people who began drinking heavily as adolescents.

Elevated liver enzymes, indicating some degree of liver damage, have been found in some adolescents who drink alcohol. Young drinkers who are overweight or obese showed elevated liver enzymes even with only moderate levels of drinking.

In both males and females, puberty is a period associated with marked hormonal changes, including increases in the sex hormones, estrogen and testosterone. These hormones, in turn, increase production of other hormones and growth factors, which are vital for normal organ development. Drinking alcohol during this period of rapid growth and development (i.e., prior to or during puberty) may upset the critical hormonal balance necessary for normal development of organs, muscles, and bones. Studies in animals also show that consuming alcohol during puberty adversely affects the maturation of the reproductive system.

Preventing Underage Drinking Within A Developmental Framework

Complex behaviors, such as the decision to begin drinking or to continue using alcohol, are the result of a dynamic interplay between genes and environment. For example, biological and physiological changes that occur during adolescence may promote risk-taking behavior, leading to early experimentation with alcohol. This behavior then shapes the child's environment, as he or she chooses friends and situations that support further drinking. Continued drinking may lead to physiological reactions, such as depression or anxiety disorders, triggering even greater alcohol use or dependence. In this way, youthful patterns of alcohol use can mark the start of a developmental pathway that may lead to abuse and dependence. Then again, not all young people who travel this pathway experience the same outcomes.

Children mature at different rates. Developmental research takes this into account, recognizing that during adolescence there are periods of rapid growth and reorganization, alternating with periods of slower growth and integration of body systems. Periods of rapid transitions, when social or. cultural factors most strongly influence the biology and behavior of the adolescent, may be the best time to target delivery of interventions. Interventions that focus on these critical development periods could alter the life course of the child, perhaps placing him or her on a path to avoid problems with alcohol.

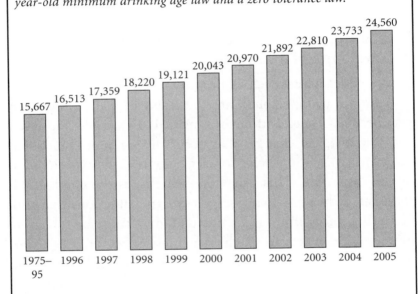

Lives Saved by MLDA 21

NHTSA [National Highway Traffic Safety Administration] estimates that minimum drinking age laws have saved 24,560 lives since 1975. In 2005 alone, these laws saved 827 lives. (Note: These lives saved represent people of all ages involving 18- to 20-year-old drivers in fatal crashes.) Every State and the District of Columbia have the 21-year-old minimum drinking age law and a zero tolerance law.

TAKEN FROM: National Highway Traffic Safety Administration, *Traffic Safety Facts, Young Drivers, 2005.*

To date, researchers have been unable to identify a single track that predicts the course of alcohol use for all or even most young people. Instead, findings provide strong evidence for wide developmental variation in drinking patterns within this special population.

Intervention Approaches

Intervention approaches typically fall into two distinct categories: (1) environmental-level interventions, which seek to reduce opportunities for underage drinking, increase penalties for violating minimum legal drinking age (MLDA) and other alcohol use laws, and reduce community tolerance for alcohol use by youth; and (2) individual-level interventions, which seek to change knowledge, expectancies, attitudes, intentions, motivation, and skills so that youth are better able to resist the pro-drinking influences and opportunities that surround them.

Environmental approaches include:

Raising the Price of Alcohol—A substantial body of research has shown that higher prices or taxes on alcoholic beverages are associated with lower levels of alcohol consumption and alcohol-related problems, especially in young people.

Increasing the Minimum Legal Drinking Age—Today all States have set the minimum legal drinking at age 21. Increasing the age at which people can legally purchase and drink alcohol has been the most successful intervention to date in reducing drinking and alcohol-related crashes among people under age 21. The National Highway Traffic Safety Administration (NHTSA) estimates that a legal drinking age of 21 saves 700 to 1,000 lives annually. Since 1976, these laws have prevented more than 21,000 traffic deaths. Just how much the legal drinking age relates to drinking-related crashes is shown by a recent study in New Zealand. Six years ago that country lowered its minimum legal drinking age to 18. Since then, alcohol-related crashes have risen 12 percent among 18- to 19-year-olds and 14 percent among 15- to 17-year-olds. Clearly a higher minimum drinking age can help to reduce crashes and save lives, especially in very young drivers.

Enacting Zero-Tolerance Laws—All States have zero-tolerance laws that make it illegal for people under age 21 to drive after any drinking. When the first eight States to adopt zero-tolerance laws were compared with nearby States without such laws, the zero-tolerance States showed a 21-percent greater decline in the proportion of single-vehicle night-time fatal crashes involving drivers under 21, the type of crash most likely to involve alcohol.

Stepping up Enforcement of Laws—Despite their demonstrated benefits, legal drinking age and zero-tolerance laws generally have not been vigorously enforced. Alcohol purchase laws aimed at sellers and buyers also can be effective, but resources must be made available for enforcing these laws.

Individual-focused interventions include:

School-Based Prevention Programs—The first school-based prevention programs were primarily informational and often used scare tactics; it was assumed that if youth understood the dangers of alcohol use, they would choose not to drink. These programs were ineffective. Today, better programs are available and often have a number of elements in common: They follow social influence models and include setting norms, addressing social pressures to drink, and teaching resistance skills. These programs also offer interactive and developmentally appropriate information, include peer-led components, and provide teacher training.

Family-Based Prevention Programs—Parents' ability to influence whether their children drink is well documented and is consistent across racial/ethnic groups. Setting clear rules against drinking, consistently enforcing those rules, and monitoring the child's behavior all help to reduce the likelihood of underage drinking. The Iowa Strengthening Families Program (ISFP), delivered when students were in grade 6, is a program that has shown long-lasting preventive effects on alcohol use.

Intervention Programs

Environmental interventions are among the recommendations included in the recent National Research Council (NRC) and Institute of Medicine (IOM) report on underage drinking. These interventions are intended to reduce commercial and social availability of alcohol and/or reduce driving while intoxicated. They use a variety of strategies, including server training and compliance checks in places that sell alcohol; deterring adults from purchasing alcohol for minors or providing alcohol to minors; restricting drinking in public places and preventing underage drinking parties; enforcing penalties for the use of false IDs, driving while intoxicated, and violating zero-tolerance laws; and raising public awareness of policies and sanctions.

The following community trials show how environmental strategies can be useful in reducing underage drinking and related problems.

The Massachusetts Saving Lives Program—This intervention was designed to reduce alcohol-impaired driving and related traffic deaths. Strategies included the use of drunk driving checkpoints, speeding and drunk driving awareness days, speed-watch telephone hotlines, high school peer-led education, and college prevention programs. The 5-year program decreased fatal crashes, particularly alcohol-related fatal crashes involving drivers ages 15–25, and reduced the proportion of 16- to 19-year-olds who reported driving after drinking, in comparison with the rest of Massachusetts. It also made teens more aware of penalties for drunk driving and for speeding.

The Community Prevention Trial Program—This program was designed to reduce alcohol-involved injuries and death. One component sought to reduce alcohol sales to minors by enforcing underage sales laws; training sales clerks, owners, and managers to prevent sales of alcohol to minors; and using the media to raise community awareness of underage drinking. Sales to apparent minors (people of legal drinking age who appear younger than age 21) were significantly reduced in the intervention communities compared with control sites.

Communities Mobilizing for Change on Alcohol—This intervention, designed to reduce the accessibility of alcoholic beverages to people under age 21, centered on policy changes among local institutions to make underage drinking less acceptable within the community. Alcohol sales to minors were reduced: 18- to 20-year-olds were less likely to try to purchase alcohol or provide it to younger teens, and the number of DUI arrests declined among 18- to 20-year-olds.

Multicomponent Comprehensive Interventions—Perhaps the strongest approach for preventing underage drinking involves the coordinated effort of all the elements that influence a child's life—including family, schools, and community. Ideally, intervention programs also should integrate treatment for youth who are alcohol dependent. Project Northland is an example of a comprehensive program that has been extensively evaluated.

Project Northland was tested in 22 school districts in northeastern Minnesota. The intervention included (1) school curricula, (2) peer leadership, (3) parental involvement programs, and (4) communitywide task force activities to address larger community norms and alcohol availability. It targeted adolescents in grades 6 through 12.

Intervention and comparison communities differed significantly in "tendency to use alcohol," a composite measure that combined items about intentions to use alcohol and actual use as well as in the likelihood of drinking "five or more in a row." Underage drinking was less prevalent in the intervention communities during phase 1; higher during the interim period (suggesting a "catch-up" effect while intervention activities were minimal); and again lower during phase 2, when intervention activities resumed.

Project Northland has been designated a model program by the Substance Abuse and Mental Health Services Administration (SAMHSA), and its materials have been adapted for a general audience. It now is being replicated in ethnically diverse urban neighborhoods.

Stopping Problems Before They Develop

Today, alcohol is widely available and aggressively promoted throughout society. And alcohol use continues to be regarded, by many people, as a normal part of growing up. Yet under-age drinking is dangerous, not only for the drinker but also for society, as evident by the number of alcohol-involved motor vehicle crashes, homicides, suicides, and other injuries.

People who begin drinking early in life run the risk of developing serious alcohol problems, including alcoholism, later in life. They also are at greater risk for a variety of adverse consequences, including risky sexual activity and poor performance in school.

Identifying adolescents at greatest risk can help stop problems before they develop. And innovative, comprehensive approaches to prevention, such as Project Northland, are showing success in reducing experimentation with alcohol as well as the problems that accompany alcohol use by young people.

> *"Drug education for teenagers should be delivered in a genuinely interactive process that promotes involvement, trust and mutual respect between young people and adults."*

Drug Education Programs Can Reduce Teen Drug Use

Rodney Skager

Rodney Skager, professor emeritus at the University of California at Los Angeles and an expert on substance abuse intervention programs, describes the downfalls associated with most drug prevention education programs and suggests solutions to make the programs more effective. He contends that drug prevention programs should provide honest and balanced information and should include interactive methods that promote student involvement, trust, and mutual respect between young people and adults.

As you read, consider the following questions:

1. Has evidence shown that drug prevention education taught to preteen children has been successful in preventing drug use in the teen years, according to the author?

Rodney Skager, "Findings and Recommendations for More Effective Drug Education for Youth: Honesty, Respect and Assistance When Needed," safety1st.org, September 30, 2004. Reproduced by permission.

2. According to Rodney Skager, is deterrent punishment effective in preventing drug use among young people?

3. Does the author believe teenagers should be consulted when developing drug prevention education programs?

These findings and recommendations [in a study performed on the effectiveness of drug education programs] propose fundamental changes in drug prevention education. First and foremost, most drug education should be moved up into secondary schools. Currently there is very little drug education for teenagers, and what there is merely repeats earlier messages that often are no longer credible to high school students. Continued wide spread use by teenagers of alcohol and other drugs suggests that "inoculating" most children against experimentation and use later on as teenagers has failed. . . .

Finding 1: Substance Use Remains Common among High School Students

For at least three decades alcohol and other drug use by peers has been widely accepted in the teen population. The majority of older teenagers, including those who choose abstinence, views use of alcohol and marijuana as a social activity. Most teenagers try alcohol or marijuana because they are curious about the effects. Young people tell us that "having fun" is the reason many peers continue to drink or use. The social climate thus engendered is tolerant of experimentation and occasional use, though not necessarily of abusive use.

Many of the negative messages delivered in drug education for preteen children become exaggerations or even falsehoods once teenagers acquire first-hand knowledge based on observations of peer use or their own experience with substances. Such experiences promote doubts about all drug information they were given as children and as a result facilitate experimentation with alcohol and other drugs. To compound the problem, older teenagers inform us that alcohol and marijuana are easy or fairly easy to obtain. There is no reason to expect that it will be more difficult in the future to obtain these drugs than it has been over the last 3 decades.

Recommendation: Prevention education and school drug policy should address this unfortunate, but real, situation. Approaches to drug education are needed for teenagers that are compatible with experience acquired in the early teen years as well as their level of cognitive and emotional development. Many teenagers are skeptical about what adults have told them about drugs. Drug education must recognize that alcohol and popular illicit drugs remain readily available to young people who choose to use them.

Finding 2: The Goal of "Inoculating" Children Against Later Alcohol and Drug Experimentation Has Been Unrealistic

Most current drug education programs are delivered to preteen children in the belief that they can be *inoculated* against later temptation. While a few programs offer booster sessions early in secondary school, these sessions merely recap earlier information and training. There is no evidence that early prevention education has been successful in preventing significant levels of alcohol and drug use by the mid teen years.

Recommendation: Drug education in elementary schools should narrow its focus to the immediate needs of children, tailored of course to the communities in which they live. For most children this includes cautions about drugs in the family medicine and liquor cabinets. It would also cover recognizing and responding to adult abuse of alcohol or other drugs, especially when it occurs in their families or immediate environment. New approaches are needed at the high school level that incorporate information on recognizing and responding to signs of drug dependency in self or others. Honest and balanced information should be provided about personal safety and how the effects of use relate to the user's state of mind and the situation in which use occurs. Information and advice

Experts Say No to Drug Testing

Physicians, social workers, substance abuse treatment providers and child advocates agree that student drug testing cannot replace pragmatic drug prevention measures, such as after-school activities. Many prominent national organizations representing these groups have come forward in court to oppose drug testing programs. These groups include the American Academy of Pediatrics, the National Education Association, the American Public Health Association, the National Association of Social Workers, and the National Council on Alcoholism and Drug Dependence. These experts have stated: "Our experience—and a broad body of relevant research—convinces us that a policy [of random student drug testing] *cannot* work in the way it is hoped to and will, for many adolescents, interfere with more sound prevention and treatment processes."

American Civil Liberties Union and the Drug Policy Alliance,
"Making Sense of Student Drug Testing:
Why Educators Are Saying No," January 2006.
www.drugpolicy.org/docUploads/drug_testing_booklet.pdf.

on personal safety does not "give permission" to drink or use drugs to those who did not ask for permission to begin with. The content and learning process of high school programs must be appropriate to the developmental level of teenagers.

Finding 3: School Punishment Policies Have Not Deterred Widespread Use of Alcohol and Other Drugs among High School Students

Education is widely viewed as the main tool for preventing drug use among young people. In reality, *deterrent* punishment currently is the fist behind the Drug Free School Zone sign. Deterrent punishment disregards the welfare of young offenders on the premise that harsh penalties such as expulsion and suspension or being barred from extracurricular activities will convince other students to remain abstinent. Yet, there is little or no evidence that deterrent punishment for the few that are caught affects the many who choose to experiment. Breaking rules set by adults is appealing to many teenagers. It can provide excitement, satisfaction and even status. Feeling connected to one's family and school is the main predictor of positive health choices among young people. Deterrent punishment destroys this sense of connection for students who experience it personally as well as for others who think it is unfair and cruel.

Recommendation: Pragmatic and humanitarian values should be the basis for all drug policy affecting young people. A public health perspective should replace deterrent punishment policies. This means that consequences for teenagers that use drugs at school or come to school under the influence of alcohol or other drugs must be embedded in a process of intervention and assistance. It does not mean that youth who commit civil violations such as selling drugs to others or driving under the influence can or should avoid criminal justice penalties. Schools that choose to adopt mandatory drug testing should (a) use the results to identify students in need of assistance and at the same time (b) avoid disadvantaging students testing positive if their behavior at school and academic performance are otherwise acceptable and there are no other signs of problematic consequences of use. In other words, those who do not need treatment should not be required to receive it. However, these students may be referred for non-punitive individual or group counseling.

Finding 4: Youth Has a Voice and It Deserves to Be Heard

Developers of prevention programs over the last three or four decades have built and rebuilt drug prevention education without consulting young people about what they now think about the prevention programs they experienced as children.

Continuing to ignore the ultimate target audience when developing programs or strategies for high school students assures failure.

Recommendation: Open and honest dialogue must go on with high school students to elicit their recollections about drug prevention education experienced in earlier grades and gain information on what they now want to know and by what process they want to learn it. "Nothing about us without us," a principle derived from the disability rights movement, applies with equal force to working with contemporary teenagers.

Finding 5: Drug Education for Teenagers Must Be Genuinely Interactive

Research has demonstrated that drug education for teenagers must use interactive teaching and learning strategies. However, there is no standard based on established principles of adolescent development that defines what this concept means in practice. Drug education programs touted by their developers as "interactive" are likely to be so to only a limited degree at best. These approaches do not meet the needs of high school students for open dialogue and integration of personal questions and experience. Drug education that is dishonest or biased cannot be genuinely interactive because young people would offer counter arguments based on experience.

Recommendation: Drug education for teenagers should be delivered in a genuinely interactive process that promotes involvement, trust and mutual respect between young people and adults. Adults who work effectively with young people acknowledge mental capacities that develop in the early teen years as well as experience that most teens acquire on their own. They are aware that development of capacity for critical thinking early in adolescence underlies skepticism that many older teens feel toward politically correct prevention messages. Honesty is a necessary condition for a truly interactive learning process. Honesty means examining both sides of all issues relating to alcohol and other drug use. Most teenagers will quickly perceive half-truths and exaggerations as just more indoctrination.

Honest drug education encourages participation by young people in setting the agenda, sharing experience, freedom to ask any question, flexibility in the order of topics, and opportunity to share responsibility for making the process a success. Adults who work with young people must be fully aware of the social world in which youth live today.

"America's most pervasive and expensive youth drug education program is (and always has been) a gigantic and incontrovertible flop."

Drug Education Programs Do Not Reduce Teen Drug Use

Paul Armentano

Paul Armentano contends in the following viewpoint that anti-drug programs for teens—specifically the Drug Abuse Resistance Education (D.A.R.E.) program—do not work. Studies have found no difference in the use of illicit drugs among those students who were D.A.R.E. graduates and those who were not. Armentano further asserts that state and federal governments should stop spending hundreds of millions of dollars on ineffective programs and should, instead, pursue a youth drug education program that might actually work. Paul Armentano is the deputy director for The NORML Foundation, a nonprofit foundation associated with the National Organization for the Reform of Marijuana Laws (NORML) that was established to educate the public about marijuana.

Paul Armentano, "The Truth About D.A.R.E.," *AlterNet*, April 4, 2003. Reproduced by permission.

As you read, consider the following questions:

1. According to the viewpoint, who teaches the D.A.R.E. program in the schools?
2. According to statistics cited in the viewpoint, do most teens engage in significant drug use?
3. Where does the money that pays for the D.A.R.E. program come from, according to the author?

If popularity were the sole measure of success then D.A.R.E., the "Drug Abuse Resistance Education" curriculum, which is now taught in 80 percent of school districts nationwide, would be triumphant. However, if one is to gauge success by actual results, then America's most pervasive and expensive youth drug education program is (and always has been) a gigantic and incontrovertible flop.

So says the General Accounting Office (GAO) in a scathing new [2003] report that finds the politically popular program has had "no statistically significant long-term effect on preventing youth illicit drug use." In addition, students who participate in D.A.R.E. demonstrate "no significant differences ... [in] attitudes toward illicit drug use [or] resistance to peer pressure" compared to children who had not been exposed to the program, the GAO determined.

Scare Tactics and "Just Say No" Ideology Do Not Work

Their critique was the latest in a long line of stinging evaluations that have plagued D.A.R.E. throughout its 20-year history. Established in 1983 by former Los Angeles police chief Daryl (All casual drug users should be taken out and shot!) Gates, the D.A.R.E. elementary school curriculum consists of 17 lessons—taught by D.A.R.E.-trained uniformed police officers—urging kids to resist the use of illicit drugs, including the underage use of alcohol and tobacco. Upon completion of the curriculum, which often relies on scare tactics and transparent "just say no" ideology, graduates "pledge to lead a drug-free life." Numerous studies indicate few do.

These include:

- A 1991 University of Kentucky study of 2,071 sixth graders that found no difference in the past-year use of cigarettes, alcohol or marijuana among D.A.R.E. graduates and non-graduates two years after completing the program.

- A 1996 University of Colorado study of over 940 elementary school students that found no difference with regard to illicit drug use, delay of experimentation with illicit drugs, self-esteem, or resistance to peer pressure among D.A.R.E. graduates and non-graduates three years after completing the program.

- A 1998 University of Illinois study of 1,798 elementary school students that found no differences with regards to the recent use of illicit drugs among D.A.R.E. graduates and non-graduates six years after completing the program.

- A 1999 follow-up study by the University of Kentucky that found no difference in lifetime, past-year, or past-month use of marijuana among D.A.R.E. graduates and non-graduates 10 years after completing the program.

Program Continues Despite Ineffectiveness

In fact, over the years so many studies have assailed D.A.R.E.'s effectiveness that by 2001 even its proponents admitted it needed serious revamping. However, rather than shelving the failed program altogether, D.A.R.E.'s advocates called for expanding its admittedly abysmal curriculum to target middle-school and high-school students—a move that was lauded by many federal officials and peer educators despite a track record that would spell the demise for most any other program.

A Culture of Drugs

Though we urge our young people to be "drug-free," the American public, including children, are perpetually bombarded with messages that encourage them to imbibe and medicate with a variety of substances. Alcohol, tobacco, caffeine, over-the-counter and prescription drugs seem to be everywhere. In fact, the *Journal of the American Medical Association* recently reported that 80% of adults in the U.S. use at least one medication every week, and half take a prescription drug. Nearly one in two American adults uses alcohol regularly; and more than one-third have tried marijuana at some time in their lives, a fact not lost on their children. . . .

Teenage drug use seems to mirror modern American drug-taking tendencies. Therefore, some psychologists have argued that given the nature of our culture, to define teenage experimentation with legal and illegal substances as "deviant" is inaccurate.

A common, though faulty, assumption driving our prevention efforts is that if teenagers simply believe that experimentation with alcohol or other drugs is dangerous, they will abstain. As a result, many programs include exaggerated risk and danger messages. Although the old *Reefer Madness*-style messages have been replaced with assertions that we now have scientific "proof" that drugs are dangerous, critical evaluations, particularly of marijuana, pierce holes in the most common assertions and are inconsistent with students' observations and experiences. Hence the cynicism we see in so many teenagers regarding the anti-drug messages they regularly receive.

Marsha Rosenbaum,
"A Reality-Based Approach to Teens and Drugs,"
National Assocation of School Psychologists (NASP)
Communiqué, *vol. 33, no. 4, 2004.*

So why does D.A.R.E. remain so immensely popular with politicians (Both Bush I [George H.W. Bush] and [Bill] Clinton endorsed "National D.A.R.E. Day.") and school administrators despite its stunning lack of demonstrated efficacy? Researchers writing in the American Psychological Association's Journal of Consulting and Clinical Psychology offer two explanations.

The first is that for many civic leaders, teaching children to refrain from drugs simply "feels good." Therefore, advocates of the program perceive any scrutiny of their effectiveness to be overly critical and unnecessary.

The second explanation is that D.A.R.E. and similar youth anti-drug education programs appear to work. After all, most kids who gradute D.A.R.E. do not engage in drug use beyond the occasional beer or marijuana cigarette. However, this reality is hardly an endorsement of D.A.R.E., but an acknowledgement of the statistical fact that most teens—even without D.A.R.E.—never engage in any significant drug use.

Anti-Drug Programs Are More Political than Successful

Of course, those looking for a third explanation could simply follow the money trail. Even though D.A.R.E. has been a failure at persuading kids to steer away from drugs, it has been a marketing cash cow, filling its coffers with hundreds of millions of dollars in annual federal aid. (According to the GAO, exact totals are unavailable but outside experts have placed this figure at anywhere from $600 [million] to $750 million per year.)

In addition, police departments spend an additional $215 million yearly on D.A.R.E. to pay for their officers' participation in the program, according to the *New York Times*. But this total may be only the tip of the iceberg. According to a preliminary economic assessment by Le Moyne College in

New York, the total economic costs of officers' training and participation in D.A.R.E. is potentially closer to $600 million.

Regardless of its ultimate financial cost to taxpayers, there is no doubt that D.A.R.E. has become its own special interest group, aggressively lobbying state and federal governments to maintain its swelling budget. Like a junkie, D.A.R.E. is addicted to the money, and will do whatever it takes to get it. Meanwhile, its proponents remain in a state of denial, caring more about political posturing than embracing a youth drug education program that really works. After 20 years of failure, isn't it about time someone dares to tell the truth?

> "Hollywood cannot underestimate the horrific toll that smoking in movies will have on the health of an entire generation," said Dr. Richard Frankenstein, president of the California Medical Association. "Research has shown that U.S. deaths attributable to youth exposure to on-screen tobacco will be greater than drunk driving, drug abuse, criminal violence and HIV/AIDS combined."

Smoking Portrayed in Movies Increases Teen Smoking

Business Wire

New research by the Los Angeles County Department of Public Health confirms the effect of smoking in movies on teens between the ages of thirteen and seventeen. Key findings include that 37 percent of teens who said they saw frequent tobacco use by actors in movies, videos, and on TV admitted that they also smoke or have tried smoking. Although there are fewer incidents of smoking in movies than there used to be, the Motion Picture Association of America has not yet changed their ratings to reflect ongo-

"L.A. County Department of Public Health Urges Hollywood to Seriously Address Movies' Impact on Teen Smoking," *Business Wire*, May 28, 2008.

ing tobacco use that still appears in films, and the Los Angeles County Department of Public Health is calling upon them to change the ratings.

As you read, consider the following questions:

1. A five-year study by scientists at Dartmouth released in 2001 suggested that an estimated what percent of tobacco use initiation is directly attributable to tobacco use in movies?

2. According to Business Wire, what is one way to reduce the negative impact of smoking scenes in movies?

3. What does the Los Angeles County Department of Public Health believe the Motion Picture Association of America should rate new movies that show ongoing tobacco use as stated in the viewpoint?

Today the Los Angeles County Department of Public Health marked the one-year anniversary of the Motion Picture Association of America's (MPAA) pledge to address the impact of smoking in movies aimed at teen audiences by calling the MPAA's efforts lackluster. Public Health, joined by representatives from the California Medical Association, University of California, San Francisco (UCSF) Smoke-free Movies Project, Breathe California Thumbs Up! Thumbs Down! Project, and the American Medical Association Alliance urged Hollywood to address the fact that smoking in movies is a powerful pro-tobacco influence on children.

Smoking in Movies Affects Teens, Studies Show

New research released by Public Health confirms the effect smoking in movies is having on California youth between 13 and 17 years of age.

Key findings include:

- Among youth who reported seeing smoking in movies occasionally or hardly ever, only 13.5 percent started smoking. That number jumped dramatically to 21.8 percent among youth who reported seeing smoking in almost all movies.

- 37 percent of teens who said they saw frequent tobacco use by actors in movies, videos and on TV admitted that they also smoke or have tried smoking.

- Among Asian-American youth who reported seeing smoking in movies occasionally or hardly ever, 11.3 percent started smoking. However, that number jumped more than three times to 38.9 percent among those who reported seeing smoking in almost all movies.

- Among Latino youth who reported seeing smoking in movies occasionally or hardly ever, 12.6 percent started smoking. That number more than doubled to 27.3 percent among those who reported seeing smoking in almost all movies.

"These findings are a disturbing affirmation of the impact of smoking in youth-rated films, especially for Latinos and Asian Americans," said Dr. Jonathan E. Fielding, MD, MPH, Public Health Director and County Health Officer. "Hollywood needs to recognize that what youth see on the big screen affects their health habits, and that the impact of smoking in movies cannot be underestimated. Eliminating tobacco use in youth-rated movies is critical in our effort to reduce the number of young people who start smoking."

Imitating Heroes

These findings are consistent with other national surveys of teen smoking behavior. A five-year study by scientists at Dartmouth released in 2001 suggests that an estimated 52 percent

Film Companies Eliminate Smoking

The Walt Disney Company recently banned images of smoking from all Disney-branded films. If smoking does appear in a future film, an anti-smoking message will appear at the beginning of the movie.

Smoke Free Movies, an organization that lobbies to rid movies of smoking, praised Disney's decision. The organization researched smoking in Disney's youth-related films from 1999 to 2006. They study found that 89 out of 138 of the films had smoking in them. "The more smoking in the movies the kids see, the more they're going to smoke. You want to reduce that," says Stanton A. Glantz, head of Smoke Free Movies. "[Movie studios] are now recognizing this is a problem. This is a baby step in the right direction."

The Motion Picture Association of America (MPAA) is also studying the issue of smoking in movies. The MPAA is considering whether to give an R rating to any movie with smoking in it.

www.weeklyreader.com, 2003.

of tobacco use initiation is directly attributable to tobacco use in movies. The study also found that adolescents who viewed their favorite movie stars smoking on the big screen were significantly more likely to imitate their heroes and become smokers themselves. The study shows these adolescents were also significantly more likely to show a greater acceptance toward smoking than adolescents who prefer non-smoking actors.

Also released today, a report by researchers from UCSF and Breathe California of Sacramento-Emigrant Trails shows that the MPAA has failed to adequately include smoking as a

factor when rating movies one year after pledging to do so. The audit of the MPAA's tobacco-rating practices found no substantial change in the percentage of G, PG, and PG-13 films with tobacco scenes since the new ratings plan was announced. While there was a reduction in the number of tobacco incidents in PG-13 movies, the percentage of youth-rated films with smoking has not decreased.

New MPAA Policies

Although there are fewer incidents of smoking in movies, MPAA has not changed their ratings to reflect on-going tobacco use that still appear in films. We are asking MPAA to adopt four policies:

1. Rating new movies that show tobacco use "R". The only exception should be when the presentation of tobacco clearly and unambiguously reflects the dangers and consequences of tobacco use or is necessary to represent the smoking of a real historical figure;

2. Certification that there were no pay-offs for using or displaying tobacco;

3. No tobacco brand identification;

4. Strong anti-smoking ads before movies with smoking.

"It is clear that Hollywood's attempt at dealing with this problem via the MPAA's tobacco-rating policy announced last year has proven to be woefully inadequate," noted Stanton Glantz, professor of medicine at UCSF. "The reality is that mainstream movies continue to deliver billions of tobacco impressions and are a strong recruiter of new teen smokers. Further delay in substantially reducing youth exposure to on-screen tobacco imagery, in full knowledge of the massive health consequences, is irresponsible and unacceptable."

Studies show that one way to reduce the negative impact of smoking scenes in movies is to expose teens to an anti-smoking message prior to watching a movie. Based on this research, Public Health is launching a new 15-second anti-smoking trailer to run in theaters this summer. The messages in the trailer are specifically tailored to resonate with young people, using a humorous approach with reasons not to smoke in youth-oriented, relatable terms. The trailer will initially run in selected theaters throughout LA County before every movie. The trailer will also be made available to air in local communities throughout California and the nation.

"Hollywood cannot underestimate the horrific toll that smoking in movies will have on the health of an entire generation," said Dr. Richard Frankenstein, president of the California Medical Association. "Research has shown that U.S. deaths attributable to youth exposure to on-screen tobacco will be greater than drunk driving, drug abuse, criminal violence and HIV/AIDS combined. The time is now to get smoking out of youth-rated films."

"No adolescent ever starts drinking or using drugs thinking he or she is going to become addicted," notes Dr. Brown. "That's the real trap of it all. Adolescents feel invincible. They feel they'll be able to control it. But before they know it, they're addicted. It's very difficult to break an addiction."

Society Needs To Be Aware of Teens' Prescription Drug Abuse

Kathiann M. Kowalski

In the following viewpoint, Kathiann M. Kowalski reveals the rising rate of prescription drug abuse by teenagers. She explains that prescription drugs are approved by the Food and Drug Administration for specific purposes only, and that they are safe only when prescribed by a physician. The number of teens who abuse prescription medication is substantial—in a 2002 survey, 10 percent of 12th graders said they had used prescription narcotics without a prescription, a category that includes medicines such as Vicodin, OxyCotin, Percocet, and Dilaudid. Abuse can begin when a friend gives away pills at school, when teens steal a couple of pills from a family member, or when teens obtain pills from a dealer. Since mixing prescriptions can be lethal, Kowalski encourages teens to be honest with their doctors about their prescription drug use. Kathiann M. Kowalski is a freelance writer and a 1974 graduate of Harvard University.

As you read, consider the following questions:

1. What percent of 12th graders had used tranquilizers, according to a 2002 Monitoring the Future survey?
2. Why is it dangerous to use somebody else's medicine?
3. What is a potential danger sign for addiction when using prescription drugs?

"Morphine Helped Cause Death of Delaware Teen," read the Columbus Dispatch headline. According to the coroner's report, a mixture of morphine and over-the-counter allergy medicine killed 15-year-old Samantha. Less than two weeks earlier, the same combination had killed a high school senior in Licking County, Ohio.

In Los Angeles, more than a dozen students at two high schools got sick after taking the stimulant Ritalin. Police later arrested five teens. They had sold or given away the pills to other students.

While prescription medicines are used legally for certain purposes, they are not safe for everyone. Abuse can kill.

By Prescription Only

Prescription drugs are medicines that have been approved by the Food and Drug Administration for specific purposes. They can be used legally only under the direction of a physician. The doctor can tell if a patient has a certain condition and can prescribe the proper dosage, based on the person's age and weight. Also, the doctor can advise the patient about possible side effects or interactions with other medicines.

Thanks to prescription medicines, doctors can effectively treat a wide range of medical conditions. Have you ever had to see the doctor for a severe headache or muscle strain? If over-the-counter pain relievers did not work, your doctor might have prescribed a stronger analgesic to reduce pain.

Opioids and opiates are another kind of pain killer. They work by attaching to certain receptors in the brain and spinal cord and blocking pain messages from going to the brain. A hospital may give morphine intravenously after surgery, for example. Or, a doctor may prescribe pills, such as Percocet, Percodan, or Darvon. (Heroin and opium are also opiates, but they have no legitimate medical use.)

Central nervous system depressants include barbiturates, such as Mebaral or Nembutal. Doctors may prescribe them for severe insomnia, or sedation while performing surgical procedures. Tranquilizers such as Xanax, Valium, and Librium are also central nervous system depressants. They help patients who suffer from severe anxiety disorders, panic attacks, or severe stress.

Stimulants are drugs that enhance brain activity and increase the body's heart and breathing rates. Stimulants can help some patients with narcolepsy (a sleeping disorder) and depression.

Stimulants can also treat ADHD (attention deficit hyperactivity disorder). Ritalin and Adderall are examples. They help young people with this condition function normally. "If the diagnosis has been made carefully, and the treatment is taken as it's prescribed, there's a very low risk of user addiction," notes Richard Brown, M.D., at the University of Wisconsin Medical School.

Prescription drugs do a lot of good when they are prescribed and used properly. Sometimes, though, people abuse them.

How Abuse Occurs

A small percentage of drug abusers start out by taking medicines that were prescribed for them. More often, however, teens who abuse these drugs take medicine that is not prescribed for them. Sometimes a "friend" gives it to them at school. Other times, they steal a couple of pills at a time from friends or family members. Or, they may buy from dealers at school, work, or elsewhere. In one recent case, Boston police arrested a teen for robbing a pharmacy at gunpoint.

Unfortunately, the number of teens who abuse prescription medicines is substantial. In the 2002 Monitoring the Future survey, 10 percent of 12th graders said they had used prescription narcotics other than under a doctor's orders. The category included medicines such as Vicodin, OxyContin, Percocet, and Dilaudid.

Similarly, 10 percent of the 12th graders surveyed had used barbiturates. Eleven percent had used tranquilizers. Within the 30 days before the survey, 4 percent had used Ritalin without a doctor's supervision.

When doctors prescribe medicines, they consider a patient's medical history, including age and weight, allergies, other medicines that the patient uses, and so forth. While the patient may still need to beware of side effects or interactions, someone who has a legitimate prescription knows it is meant for him or her and can feel confident that the medicine is what it is supposed to be.

Teens who take drugs that were not prescribed for them cannot be sure what they are. If a 120-pound teen steals a pill meant for a 220-pound man, that teen risks a serious overdose. That's why it's dangerous to use someone else's medicine.

"People should be especially cautious if they have some kind of ongoing medical problem," notes Dr. Brown. "They may not be aware that a certain medication may be dangerous for them."

Drug Interactions and Reactions

Some medicines interact with other drugs. Some trigger serious allergic reactions.

Different drugs present specific health risks. Tranquilizers, barbiturates, and narcotics all slow the central nervous system. Potential health consequences include confusion, memory problems, loss of coordination, and impaired judgment. Depressants can also cause dangerously slow breathing, coma, and even death.

Stimulants speed up the central nervous system. Undesirable side effects can include sleep disorders, irritability, aggression, and hyperactivity. More serious health consequences can include irregular heartbeat, elevated body temperature, and fatal seizures or heart attacks.

Mixing prescription drugs with each other, with alcohol, or with other drugs multiplies their risks. Doctors call this a synergistic effect. Even though the allergy pills that Samantha took were over-the-counter medicine, the depressant in them magnified the potent effects of the morphine.

With their judgment impaired, teens are also more likely to engage in risky behavior. That includes impaired driving, sexual activity, and criminal behavior. Accidents, injuries, HIV and other sexually transmitted diseases, pregnancies, and arrests all become more likely.

Addiction: A Downward Spiral

Beyond their immediate health risks, many prescription medicines are also addictive. "Usually when people with legitimate medical conditions take these medicines, they don't feel euphoria. They feel relief of symptoms," says Dr. Brown. "But when someone who doesn't have a legitimate medical problem takes them, they feel the effects much more, and that leads to more use. Eventually, when kids take enough of the medicine and if they have a genetic predisposition, they can end up addicted." No one can know beforehand whether or not he or she has a genetic predisposition to become addicted to any drug.

"Prolonged use of these drugs eventually changes the brain in fundamental and long-lasting ways, which explains why people cannot just quit on their own, and why treatment is essential," Glen Hanson of the National Institute on Drug Abuse explained to a Senate committee last year. "In effect, drugs of abuse take over the brain's normal pleasure and motivational systems, moving drug use to the highest priority, thereby overriding all other motivations and drives. These brain changes are responsible for the compulsion to seek and use drugs that we have come to define as addiction."

As people become addicted, their lives spiral downward, out of control. They steal or incur debts to maintain their habit. Performance in school and work drops. Personal relationships deteriorate.

"No adolescent ever starts drinking or using drugs thinking he or she is going to become addicted," notes Dr. Brown. "That's the real trap of it all. Adolescents feel invincible. They feel they'll be able to control it. But before they know it, they're addicted. It's very difficult to break an addiction."

Complications arise when some teens who start out with valid medical problems become addicted. The addiction needs to be dealt with, but the underlying medical problem may still need attention. "Often we can find other medicines that are less addictive, tighten up supervision under which they're administered, and provide mainstream addiction treatment along with some more specialized treatment for the legitimate medical diagnosis," notes Dr. Brown.

Face to Face with Your Doctor

You know prescription medicines can help a lot of health problems. But you also know now that some medicines can cause addiction. What should you do when you see the doctor?

First of all, be completely honest. If you have any history of using alcohol or other drugs, say so. Don't assume that the doctor can figure it out or doesn't need to know. If a teen complaining about severe anxiety uses alcohol, for example, the doctor may decide not to prescribe certain tranquilizers. Also tell your physician about any addiction issues in the family.

Ideally, you'll be able to see your doctor one-on-one, so you can speak more freely. Most doctors will respect a teen's confidentiality. If you have any concerns, ask upfront. Doctors aren't in the business of judging patients, but helping them.

Also tell the doctor about all medicines you take—both by prescription and over-the-counter. Even vitamins or herbal supplements can interact dangerously with medications.

Be honest about your symptoms. No one else can tell you how much pain you should or shouldn't feel. Pain is a subjective experience. Too often, teens with chronic diseases such as sickle cell anemia or arthritis may suffer more than necessary.

Ask a lot of questions too. Exactly what is the medicine, and how is it supposed to work? What is the dosage? What if you forget a dose? Should you take the medicine with food? What side effects might you expect, and how should you deal with them? Should you take all of the medicine until it's gone, as doctors recommend for antibiotics? Or, should you use the medicine only as needed? Often it helps to take notes.

If a particular medicine gives you a really good feeling, tell your doctor. Feeling euphoria (as opposed to just relief of symptoms) is a potential danger sign for addiction.

On the other hand, a medicine may make you groggy or have other bad side effects. It may not be the right medicine for you. Sixteen-year-old Chris got morphine at the hospital after his arm surgery. When that made him sick, the doctor gave him Percocet instead.

"It took the pain away within minutes and lasted several hours," recalls Chris. "The only thing that I did not like was that all I wanted to do was sleep." The doctor then put him on Vicodin. Once he got home, however, Chris did not need the strong medicine. He was able to manage by taking ibuprofen and icing his shoulder instead.

Medicine is supposed to help you function better, not worse. If one medicine is not right for you, another one may work better. Your doctor might also recommend non-drug treatments, such as using ice or heat.

Be responsible with your medicines. Never share them with anyone. Even if a medicine is right for you, it could harm someone else. At home, store your medicines out of sight.

Last but not least, take any medicines exactly as prescribed. After all, that's just what the doctor ordered.

The Dangers of OxyContin

When OxyContin went on the market in 1995, the drugmaker promoted it to doctors as a relatively safe narcotic. The round pills had a time-release mechanism for their synthetic version of morphine, oxycodone. Instead of giving patients a euphoric high, the drug could provide strong and sustained pain relief for chronic conditions like cancer and arthritis.

Soon, however, abusers looking for a quick high began chewing tablets or snorting crushed pills. Others dissolved them in water and injected the mixture. These methods quickly put dangerously high levels of oxycodone into the bloodstream.

OxyContin is known by the street names "oxy," "oxy-cotton," and "hillbilly heroin." In some rural areas, large numbers of people became addicted.

Abuse spread from rural areas to suburbs and cities. Oxy-Contin became the subject of serious fraud, theft, and drug trafficking problems. Meanwhile, some patients who really needed the medicine had trouble getting it.

OxyContin abuse has killed many people, including teenagers. The Drug Enforcement Agency estimated that OxyContin played a part in more than 460 deaths during a two-year period.

The drug's maker has been working on a newer version. An added ingredient would block the drug's effect if someone chewed or crushed the pill. But the new version is not available yet. Meanwhile, the company has been named in more than a dozen lawsuits.

The bottom line? Experimenting with drug abuse is always dangerous.

Over-the-Counter Drugs Can Pose Risks Too

You don't need a prescription to buy over-the-counter (OTC) medicines. Yet they can still present risks.

Some cough and cold medicines contain alcohol or other depressants. Other medicines have decongestants that speed up the heart rate. Still other medicines may contain both kinds of drugs.

Abusing these medicines to get a high or spaced-out feeling can be dangerous. Mixing them with alcohol, prescription medicines, or other drugs is even more risky.

Periodical Bibliography

The following articles have been selected to supplement the diverse views presented in this chapter.

American Cancer Society	"How to Fight Teen Smoking," www.cancer.org, 2007.
Associated Press	"Survey: Some Teens See Little Risk in Meth Use," FoxNews.com, September 19, 2007.
Greg Cima	"Should the Drinking Age Be Lowered to 18 from 21?" pantagraph.com, September 15, 2007.
William V. Corr	"Testimony Before House Health Subcommittee in Support of FDA Regulation of Tobacco Products," TobaccoFreeKids.org, October 3, 2007.
Education.com	"Teenage Smoking Not Declining as Fast as Usual: A Call to Parents and Washington," 2007.
Katherine Francis	"Tobacco Tax Needed to Prevent Teen Smoking," Council of Community Clinics, September 26, 2006.
Miranda Hitti	"Smoking in Movies May Tempt Kids," ReachOut.com, June 30, 2007.
Alex Johnson	"Debate on Lower Drinking Age Bubbling Up: Proponents Say Current Restriction Drives Teen Alcohol Use Underground," MSNBC.com, August 14, 2007.
National Institute on Drug Abuse (NIDA)	"Prescription Drugs: Abuse and Addiction," drugabuse.gov, August 2005.
Newsweek.com	"Smokin' in the Boys (and Girls) Room," 2007.
Todd Zwillich	"Report: Cold Drugs Used to Get High," WebMD.com, January 10, 2008.

For Further Discussion

Chapter 1

1. Finessa Ferrell-Smith contends that bullying is a problem in schools and can produce serious consequences for both the victim and the bully. Matthew S. Robinson reveals that gay and lesbian youth are often the victims of such bullying. Do you think that schools need to implement stricter policies against those students who bully or harass their classmates? Why or why not?

2. B. Timothy Walsh and V. L. Cameron contend that one of the reasons teens develop eating disorders is dissatisfaction with their physical appearance. Do you believe that society puts too much emphasis on being thin? Explain your answer.

3. Matthew S. Robinson points out the harassment and bullying that gay teens receive at school. Gay-straight alliances and other organizations at school can offer support to LGBT students. What are the challenges of these groups, and how can they be supportive to teens?

Chapter 2

1. According to Emma Elliott, comprehensive sex education programs give teenagers a false sense of security by teaching "safe-sex" practices. Considering the high rate of sexually transmitted diseases and the failure rates of condoms and contraceptives, she contends that "safe sex" does not exist and that teenagers should be taught abstinence sex education. On the other hand, Arthur Caplan maintains that teens are going to have sex regardless of abstinence sex education programs, so they need medical

and scientific information about sex to enable them to make smart choices. Whose argument do you find more convincing? Explain your answer.

2. Cynthia Dailard and Chinue Turner Richardson contend that teenage girls have a constitutional right to obtain an abortion without parental consent. Teresa Stanton Collett asserts that parental consent should be mandatory before a teenager can obtain an abortion. Citing from the texts, explain which argument you agree with.

Chapter 3

1. Bert H. Deixler argues that gun control legislation reduces the number of deaths and injuries to American youth. Peter J. Ferrara contends that gun control legislation does not reduce gun violence, but actually increases it. After reading the arguments, whose evidence do you find more compelling? Explain.

2. Randall G. Shelden asserts that zero tolerance policies are unfair to students. But the American Psychological Association contends that zero tolerance policies can be effective if applied with greater flexibility. Citing examples from the viewpoints, which author do you think makes a better argument? Do you believe zero tolerance laws are effective and necessary in schools?

3. Congressman J. Randy Forbes argues that mandatory minimum sentences are necessary to deter gang violence. Robert C. Scott contends that mandatory sentences are unjust and counterproductive. How great an impact do you think mandatory sentencing has on preventing gang violence? Explain your answer.

Chapter 4

1. The organization Choose Responsibility and the U.S. Department of Health and Human Services debate whether

the minimum drinking age of twenty-one should be lowered. Which argument do you support, and why?

2. Paul Armentano contends that the Drug Abuse Resistance Education (D.A.R.E.) program is not effective in reducing teen drug use. Rodney Skager admits that many drug prevention programs do not work, but maintains that specific revisions can make them more effective. How might the authors' backgrounds and affiliations shape their arguments? Are these affiliations important in evaluating the opposing views?

3. Research by the Los Angeles County Department of Health, confirms the effect of smoking in movies on teens between the ages of thirteen and seventeen. How do you view smoking in movies, and what, if anything, do you think should be done about it?

Organizations to Contact

Advocates for Youth
2000 M St. NW, Suite 750, Washington, DC   20036
(202) 419-3420 • fax: (202) 419-1448
e-mail: information@advocatesforyouth.org
Web site: www.advocatesforyouth.org

Advocates for Youth believes young people should have access to information and services that help prevent teen pregnancy and the spread of sexually transmitted diseases and enable youth to make healthy decisions about sexuality. The organization publishes brochures, fact sheets, and bibliographies on adolescent pregnancy, adolescent sexuality, and sexuality education.

Afterschool Alliance
1616 H St. NW, Washington, DC   20006
(202) 347-1002
e-mail: info@afterschoolalliance.org
Web site: www.afterschoolalliance.org

The Afterschool Alliance is a nonprofit organization dedicated to raising awareness of the importance of after-school programs and advocating for quality, affordable programs for all children. The alliance provides links to numerous organizations and clearinghouses of information on after-school programs and issues. Among its publications are *Policy News* and the *Afterschool Action Kit*, which gives advice on finding or starting a quality after-school program.

Alan Guttmacher Institute
125 Maiden Ln., 7th Floor, New York, NY   10038
(212) 248-1111 • fax: (212) 248-1951
e-mail: info@guttmacher.org
Web site: www.guttmacher.org

The institute works to protect and expand the reproductive choices of all women and men. It strives to ensure people's access to the information and services they need to exercise their rights and responsibilities concerning sexual activity, reproduction, and family planning. Among the institute's publications are the fact sheet "Facts on Contraceptive Use" and the periodical "Perspectives on Sexual and Reproductive Health."

American Academy of Child and Adolescent Psychiatry (AACAP)
3615 Wisconsin Ave. NW, Washington, DC   20016-3007
(202) 966-7300 • fax: (202) 966-2891
Web site: www.aacap.org

AACAP is a nonprofit organization dedicated to providing parents and families with information regarding developmental, behavioral, and mental disorders that affect children and adolescents. The organization provides national public information through the distribution of the newsletter *Facts for Families* and the monthly *Journal of the American Academy of Child and Adolescent Psychiatry.*

American Civil Liberties Union (ACLU)
125 Broad St., 18th Floor, New York, NY   10004
Web site: www.aclu.org

The ACLU is a national organization that works to defend Americans' civil rights as guaranteed by the U.S. Constitution. It opposes curfew laws for juveniles and others and seeks to protect the public-assembly rights of gang members or people associated with gangs. The ACLU's numerous publications include the report *Making Sense of Student Drug Testing: Why Educators Are Saying No* and the brochure *HIV & Your Civil Rights.*

Anorexia Nervosa and Related Eating Disorders, Inc. (ANRED)
PO Box 5102, Eugene, OR   97405
(503) 344-1144
Web site: www.anred.com

ANRED is a nonprofit organization that provides information about anorexia nervosa, bulimia nervosa, binge-eating disorder, compulsive exercising, and other lesser-known food and weight disorders, including details about recovery and prevention. ANRED offers workshops, individual and professional training, as well as local community education. It provides links to books, articles, and other personal stories written by people who have overcome eating disorders.

Children's Defense Fund (CDF)
25 E St. NW, Washington, DC   20001
(800) 233-1200
e-mail: cdfinfo@childrensdefense.org
Web site: www.childrensdefense.org

The CDF advocates policies and programs to improve the lives of children and teens in America. CDF's Safe Start program works to prevent the spread of violence and guns in schools, and Healthy Start works for universal health care for children. The fund publishes a monthly newsletter, CDF Reports, as well as online news and reports such as *The State of America's Children* and *Protect Children, Not Guns*.

Child Trends, Inc. (CT)
4301 Connecticut Ave. NW, Suite 350
Washington, DC   20008
(202) 572-6000 • fax: (202) 362-8420
e-mail: npizarro@childtrends.org
Web site: www.childtrends.org

CT works to provide accurate statistical and research information regarding children and their families in the United States, and to educate the American public on the ways existing social trends affect children. In addition to the newsletter *Facts at a Glance*, which presents the latest data on sexual behavior and teen pregnancy for every state, CT also publishes the fact sheets *Contraceptive Use Patterns Across Sexual Relationships* and *Neighborhood Support and Children's Connectedness*.

Coalition for Juvenile Justice (CJJ)
1710 Rhode Island Ave. NW, 10th Floor
Washington, DC   20036
(202) 467-0864 • fax: (202) 887-0738
e-mail: info@juvjustice.org
Web site: www.juvjustice.org

CJJ seeks to improve the circumstances of vulnerable and troubled children, youth, and families involved with the courts and to build safe communities. In addition, the CJJ informs policy makers, advocates, and the public about the interplay of prevention, rehabilitation, and accountability in reducing juvenile crime and delinquency. Among the coalition's publications are position papers, reports, the monthly *Juvenile Justice e-Monitor*, and fact sheets, including *Alternatives to Detention in the Juvenile Justice System* and *Conditions of Confinement for Young Offenders*.

Family Research Council
801 G St. NW, Washington, DC   20001
(202) 393-2100 • fax: (202) 393-2134
Web site: www.frc.org

The council seeks to promote and protect the interest of the traditional family. It focuses on issues such as parental autonomy and responsibility, community supports for single parents, and adolescent pregnancy. Among the council's numerous publications are the papers "The Government's Profound Interest in Protecting Children" and "Media Exposure Linked to Adolescent Sex."

National Campaign to Prevent Teen Pregnancy
1776 Massachusetts Ave. NW, Suite 200
Washington, DC   20036
(202) 478-8500 • fax: (202) 478-8588
e-mail: campaign@thenc.org
Web site: www.teenpregnancy.org

The goal of the National Campaign to Prevent Teen Pregnancy is to prevent teen pregnancy by supporting values and stimulating actions that are consistent with a pregnancy-free adolescence. The organization publishes reports and fact sheets on teen attitudes, behaviors, and contraceptive use, including *Where and When Teens First Have Sex* and *The Sexual Behavior of Young Adolescents*.

National Council on Alcoholism and Drug Dependence (NCADD)

244 East 58th St., 4th Floor, New York, NY 10022
(212) 269-7797 • fax: (212) 269-7510
e-mail: national@ncadd.org
Web site: www.ncadd.org

In addition to helping individuals overcome addictions, NCADD advises the federal government on drug and alcohol policies and develops substance abuse prevention and education programs for youth. It publishes fact sheets and pamphlets on substance abuse, including the titles, *What Can You Do About Someone Else's Drinking?* and *Who's Got the Power? You. . .or Drugs?*

National Institute of Justice (NIJ)

810 Seventh St. NW, Washington, DC 20531
(202) 307-2942 • fax: (202) 307-6394
Web site: www.ojp.usdoj.gov

NIJ is the primary federal sponsor of research on crime and its control. It sponsors research efforts through grants and contracts that are carried out by universities, private institutions, and state and local agencies. Its publications include the research briefs *Toward Safe and Orderly Schools—The National Study of Delinquency Prevention in Schools* and *Commercial Sexual Exploitation of Children: What Do We Know and What Do We Do About It?*

Office of Juvenile Justice and Delinquency Prevention (OJJDP)

810 Seventh St. NW, Washington, DC 20531
(202) 307-5911
Web site: www.ojjdp.ncjrs.org

As the primary federal agency charged with monitoring and improving the juvenile justice system, the OJJDP develops and funds programs on juvenile justice. Among its goals are the prevention and control of illegal drug use and serious crime by juveniles. The OJJDP publishes a bimonthly newsletter *OJJDP News @ a Glance*, the journal *Juvenile Justice*, bulletins, including "Lessons Learned from Safe Kids/Safe Streets," and reports, including "America's Children: Key National Indicators of Well-Being."

Parents, Families, and Friends of Lesbians and Gays (PFLAG)

1726 M St. NW, Suite 400, Washington, DC 20036
(202) 467-8180 • fax: (202) 467-8194
e-mail: info@pflag.org
Web site: www.pflag.org

PFLAG promotes the health and well-being of gay, lesbian, bisexual, and transgender persons, their families, and friends through support, education, and advocacy to end discrimination and to secure equal civil rights. Among the organization's publications are the booklets *Our Daughters and Sons: Questions and Answers for Parents of Gay, Lesbian and Bisexual People* and *Be Yourself: Questions and Answers for Gay, Lesbian, Bisexual and Transgender Youth.*

Bibliography of Books

Gerald R. Adams and Michael D. Berzonsky, eds.
Blackwell Handbook of Adolescence. Malden, MA: Blackwell, 2003.

Cecilia Breinbauer
Youth: Choices and Change: Promoting Healthy Behaviors in Adolescents. Washington, DC: Pan American Health Organization, 2005.

N.H. Cambron-McCabe, M.M. McCarthy, and S.B. Thomas
Public School Law: Teachers' and Students' Rights, 5th edition. Boston: Pearson, 2004.

Michael A. Corriero
Judging Children as Children: A Proposal for a Juvenile Justice System. Philadelphia: Temple University Press, 2007.

J. Shoshanna Ehrlich
Who Decides? The Abortion Rights of Teens. Westport, CT: Praeger, 2006.

Robert Epstein
The Case Against Adolescence: Rediscovering the Adult in Every Teen. Sanger, CA: Quill Driver, 2007.

Rhett Godfrey
The Teen Code: How to Talk to Them About Sex, Drugs, and Everything Else—Teenagers Reveal What Works Best. New York: Rodale, 2004.

Gina Guddat
Unwrapped: Real Questions Asked by Real Girls (About Sex). Houston: Providence, 2007.

Marya Hornbacher — *Wasted: A Memoir of Anorexia and Bulimia.* New York: Harper Perennial, 2006.

V. Jones and L. Jones — *Comprehensive Classroom Management: Creating Communities of Support and Solving Problems,* 7th ed. Boston: Allyn and Bacon, 2004.

Karen R. Koenig — *The Rules of "Normal" Eating: A Commonsense Approach for Dieters, Overeaters, Undereaters, Emotional Eaters, and Everyone in Between!* Carlsbad, CA: Gurze, 2005.

Abigail A. Kohn — *Shooters: Myths and Realities of America's Gun Cultures.* New York: Oxford University Press, 2004.

David L. Meyers — *Boys Among Men: Trying and Sentencing Juveniles as Adults.* Westport, CT: Praeger, 2005.

Christie Pettit — *Empty: A Story of Anorexia.* Grand Rapids, MI: Revell, 2006.

Albert R. Roberts — *Juvenile Justice Sourcebook: Past, Present, and Future.* New York: Oxford University Press, 2004.

Marsha Rosenbaum — *Safety First: A Reality-Based Approach to Teens and Drugs.* San Francisco: Drug Policy Alliance, 2007.

Ritch C. Savin-Williams — *The New Gay Teenager.* Cambridge, MA: Harvard University Press, 2006.

| Laurie Schaffner | *Girls in Trouble with the Law.* Piscataway, NJ: Rutgers University Press, 2006. |

Randall G. Shelden — *Delinquency and Juvenile Justice in America.* Long Grove, IL: Waveland, 2006.

Elaine Slavens — *Peer Pressure: Deal with It Without Losing Your Cool.* Halifax, Canada: Lorimer, 2004.

Irving A. Spergel — *Reducing Youth Gang Violence: The Little Village Gang Project in Chicago.* Lanham, MD: AltaMira, 2006.

L. Steinberg — *Adolescence.* New York: McGraw-Hill, 2005.

Jason Stone and Andrea Stone — *The Drug Dilemma: Responding to a Growing Crisis.* New York: IDEA, 2003.

Barbara Strauch — *Primal Teen: What the New Discoveries About the Teenage Brain Tell Us About Our Kids.* New York: Bantam Doubleday, 2004.

B. Timothy Walsh and V.L. Cameron — *If Your Adolescent Has an Eating Disorder: An Essential Resource for Parents.* New York: Oxford University Press, 2005.

David Walsh — *Why Do They Act That Way? A Survival Guide to the Adolescent Brain for You and Your Teen.* New York: Simon & Schuster, 2005.

| David A. Wolfe, Peter G. Jaffe, and Claire V. Crooks | *Adolescent Risk Behaviors: Why Teens Experiment and Strategies to Keep Them Safe.* New Haven, CT: Yale University Press, 2006. |

Index